1. **This book may be kept three weeks. It is to be returned on / before the last date stamped below.**
2. **A fine of 25c will be charged for every week or part of week a book is overdue.**

....		....
....		....
....	FOR	....
....	Ref	....
....	only	....
....		....
....		....
....		....
....		....
....		....
....		....

Driving the Tiger
Irish Enterprise Spirit

Driving the Tiger
Irish Enterprise Spirit

John J. Travers

Gill & Macmillan Ltd

Gill & Macmillan Ltd
Hume Avenue
Park West
Dublin 12
with associated companies throughout the world
www.gillmacmillan.ie

© 2001 John Travers
0 7171 3303 6
Design by Carole Lynch, Dublin.
Print origination by Linda Kelly, Dublin.
Printed by ColourBooks, Dublin.
Cover photograph of Moya Doherty
courtesy of Declan Doherty of the *Derry People*.

The paper used in this book is made from the wood pulp of managed forests. For every tree felled, at least one tree is planted, thereby renewing natural resources.

A catalogue record is available for this book from the British Library.

54321

For Isla

CONTENTS

ACKNOWLEDGMENTS

It is a great pleasure to thank Ciara Sherlock for her help, without which this book could not have been completed. Ciara conducted final interviews with featured enterprise leaders after I left Dublin to begin my studies in Boston and she also researched the photographs. Her professionalism, support and good humour contributed largely to making this project so enjoyable.

Many thanks to my good friend John McManus and also to Brenda O'Hanlon and Brendan O'Kelly for their encouragement. I owe special thanks to Michael Gill for his expert guidance in developing this book and in bringing it to publication. Deirdre Greenan, Pamela Coyle, Patricia Hannon and the production team at Gill & Macmillan and Priscilla O'Connor contributed great time and effort to making this book a reality.

I am very happy to thank the following people who helped in arranging and preparing interviews: Giselle Davies and Ros Ryder (Jordan Formula 1); Olivia Gaynor and Gavin Marrow (Parthus); Una Rickard (Aer Arann); Gerry Lundberg and Sinead O'Doherty (Tyrone Productions); Sally-Anne McEvoy, Nicola Prendergast and Lynn Farrell (Communicorp); Evelyn Gaffney, Ruth Burrows, Carol Grogan and Ciaran O'Connell (IONA Technologies); Valerie Ivers (Trintech); Paul Brady (Belvedere Youth Club); Niall Morris (Inner City Enterprise).

Richard Linder and Tony Deifell have been especially helpful to me. Lastly, thanks in every way to John, Mary, Sharon, Penny, Fióna and Roaslind.

John J. Travers
Cambridge MA
June 2001

INTRODUCTION

I

Waves

In the most westerly cottage on Ireland's Bere Island, at the ragged periphery of Western Europe, perspective comes easily. I have come here to reflect on a series of taped interviews conducted recently with people who are shaping the future of Irish society through their enterprise.

Below the cottage, at the water's edge, the waves surge against the shore in a relentless cycle. Movements that change a society are like waves that surge, retreat and leave a new equilibrium in their wake. Whether political, economic, cultural or religious in nature, they usher in brief or prolonged periods of prosperity and international influence, or indeed the very opposite.

Italy provides a striking example of such ebb and flow over time. It saw the rise and fall of the Roman Empire, the political, social and architectural legacy of which shaped modern Europe. It witnessed the advent and decline of a new, politically autonomous entity – the city state – several of which became the first trading pivots between Western Europe and the Byzantine and Islamic Empires. During the Renaissance the patronage of the merchant class of these city states cradled the rebirth of, and unprecedented advances in, art, sculpture and architecture. Thereafter, Italy began a slow decline into relative obscurity, although in the twentieth century it has flourished once again as a world centre for avant-garde style in clothes and cars.

Ireland has enjoyed its own brief and shining periods, when heightened cultural and religious activity has influenced other nations. Almost 1,500 years ago, Ireland was the 'Island of Saints and Scholars'. Huns, Vandals and Visigoths had put an end to the social order of the Roman Empire and imposed a political, economic and cultural darkness throughout Europe. Remote Ireland, where the advent of Christianity had produced a monastic culture of great intellectual and artistic refinement, became a refuge where learning was kept alive. Until Europe's recovery under Charlemagne, Ireland was a centre of philosophical and theological thought from which mainland Europe took inspiration.

One hundred years ago, towards the end of the nineteenth century, Ireland experienced another powerful movement. Three major developments converged to form a wave of cultural revival.

The first element in this revival was what was initially called the 'Gaelic Athletic Association for the Preservation and Cultivation of National Pastimes', founded in 1884 by Michael Cusack and P.W. Nally. Both Cusack, a schoolteacher from Co. Clare, and Nally, from a Mayo farming family, were avid and accomplished athletes. They shared a desire to promote Gaelic sports and especially to encourage working-class participation. In Cusack's words, the GAA 'swept the country like a prairie fire'. The location of its clubs in parish and county units gave rise to a new local and national pride and spirit across Ireland. One commentator noted that 'the country was soon humming with interest and activity'.

The second element, the Gaelic League, was founded by Douglas Hyde and Eoin MacNeill in 1893. MacNeill, an Irish scholar from Co. Antrim, and Hyde, a Roscommon-born language scholar and writer who was later to become Ireland's first president (1937–45), wanted to preserve Irish as a national language and encourage the study of Irish literature under the auspices of the League. By 1904 the Gaelic League had enlisted some 50,000 members, and supporters initiated more than 600 branches throughout the country.

The final element was known as the Irish Literary Revival, or the Anglo-Irish Literary Renaissance. The founders of this movement, including W.B. Yeats, Maud Gonne, Douglas Hyde and Lady Gregory, outlined in their charter how they were determined 'to build up a national tradition, a national literature, which shall be nonetheless Irish in spirit for being English in language'. The literary revival produced a powerful body of literature that moulded emotion and cultural enthusiasm in a generation of Irish men and women. Anglo-Irish literature and drama attracted widespread international interest. This interest was promoted by the acting ability of the players of the Abbey Theatre (established in Dublin in 1904), who performed in theatres throughout Britain and the United States.

The confluence of these three elements of cultural revival gave rise directly to a surge of enthusiasm and national confidence. This wave began when people with exceptional vision and ability in sports, language and literature overcame the inhibitions and constraints of their past and their environment. In doing so, they fostered a new spirit of cultural vitality in Ireland.

Today, another wave of change is transforming the attitude of a generation of Irish men and women. It is contributing to the increasing prosperity of Ireland and raising the standards of living for most of the country's inhabitants. Attracting thousands of foreign workers to fill newly created job opportunities and share their wealth of diversity, it underlies Ireland's example to nations throughout the world on how to transform a modestly performing economy into a 'Celtic Tiger'. It is 'Irish Enterprise Spirit'.

II
Environment and conditions

Irish people have always demonstrated a strong enterprise spirit in the various countries to which they have emigrated over the centuries, but in Ireland itself, that spirit has lain dormant in the absence of the right environment and conditions. Ireland effectively missed two industrial revolutions: it had neither the natural resources, such as coal and pig iron, to be part of the first, characterized by steam and steel, nor the infrastructure and geographic connectivity to be part of the second, characterized by Fordist mass production. Today, however, Ireland has the resources to play a full part in the third industrial revolution, characterized by information technology and a new economy that transcends the limits of geography and physical assets.

The crafting of economic policy in Ireland from the foundation of the state until the 1990s provided fertile ground for an enterprise spirit to take root, and the confluence of several important conditions – both domestic and global – enabled this spirit to grow and flourish.

Turning the soil – Evolution of the Irish economy
Following a brief flirtation with laissez-faire economic policies after Irish independence in 1922, there was a decisive shift towards protectionism and national self-sufficiency. This was in line with contemporary economic thinking. John Maynard Keynes, for example, in a lecture delivered in Dublin in 1933, advised his audience, 'Let goods be homespun wherever it is reasonably possible, and above all, let finance be primarily national.' Against a backdrop of world economic depression, this policy gave rise to only limited success. National electrification and a transport infrastructure for rail, bus, sea

and air were established by the state. However, labour productivity fell in the protected environment, and the labour force declined through mass emigration from an under-industrialized, agriculture-dependent state.

The impact of the failed protectionist polices became clear in the 1961 census of population. This indicated that the population, at 2.8 million, had fallen to its lowest level for some 200 years. These sombre developments drove a shift in policy to outward orientation of the economy in the 1950s and 1960s. Measures included promotion of foreign direct investment (FDI) and a moratorium on corporation tax on profits from export activity. The results of this shift towards internationalism were significantly beneficial. Gross domestic product (GDP) grew at an average rate of 4.5% per year over the period 1960–73. The decline in population was arrested, and living standards rose.

With membership of the EEC in 1973, expectations for continued economic development were high. In the event, these expectations were not realized during the 1970s and 1980s. Stimulation of the economy through high public-sector borrowing and spending by successive governments was unsustainable. The statistics painted a grim picture: the national debt increased as a proportion of gross national product (GNP) from 67% in 1973 to 105% in 1983. Taxation as a proportion of GNP increased from 31% in 1973 to 42% in 1985, and unemployment rose to over 16%.

By the mid-1980s, the Irish economy was in deep crisis. The crisis forced the setting aside of sectional interests and the agreement of a Programme for National Recovery between government, employers and trade unions. Industrial development policy continued to encourage a high-tech, knowledge-based, export-driven economy.

These economic developments have led to a period of exceptional economic growth in Ireland in the 1990s. The average annual rate of increase in GDP has been 9%, outstripping the European average by a factor of three. Unemployment has fallen from 16% in 1993 to under 4% in 2001. Over the same period of time, the debt/GNP ratio has fallen from just over 90% to below 40%. Ireland has established itself as one of the most open and competitive trading economies in the world.

The right conditions – Fostering a spirit of enterprise

Europe's fastest-growing economy throughout the 1990s provided natural opportunities for people to undertake new enterprise initiatives. But even in this favourable environment, several important conditions facilitated the growth of an enterprise spirit

A key condition is significant foreign direct investment in Ireland. The Institute for Management Development (IMD) in Switzerland ranked Ireland seventh in the world in terms of competitiveness for business in its World Competitiveness Scoreboard 2001. Dozens of multinational, high-tech companies have taken advantage by establishing European bases in Ireland. Their arrival has given rise to the need for spin-off enterprise initiatives in areas such as construction, logistics and catering. Employment by the multinationals and resultant increased consumer spending has created a demand for new services, retail and entertainment enterprise. Foreign companies have also brought with them a wealth of ideas and knowledge, particularly in the area of advanced technology, that has inspired the creation of indigenous high-tech enterprises. The culture of global success that foreign companies have brought with them has contributed to a new sense of 'anything is possible' in enterprise. Best-practice management and organizational models have been introduced to Ireland and have contributed to a productivity growth that has been measured by the OECD to be five times the European average and two and a half times the US average throughout the 1990s.

A second major condition is an abundance of funds made available for the promotion of enterprise in Ireland. US firms alone have invested some $3.5 billion a year in business initiatives, yielding these firms the highest rate of return compared to investments in all other European countries, according to the US Department of Commerce. An unprecedented total of some £4 billion was spent on research and development in the 1990s, with significant amounts made available by the Irish government to 'first time' research and development performers. Ireland has been placed firmly on the agenda of international venture capitalists seeking to invest in new start-up ventures, and the indigenous venture capital sector has grown strongly and become more sophisticated and professional. High-profile international stock market flotation of companies such as CBT, Iona and Trintech has heightened investors' awareness of the potential of enterprising Irish companies. Finally, successful Irish enterprise leaders are themselves making significant investments in indigenous Irish enterprises, making funds available to like-minded people wishing to test their entrepreneurial skills in the marketplace.

A third condition that has encouraged enterprise in Ireland is the vast improvement in education over the last generation. Since 1980, the proportion of the population attaining third-level education has doubled, to more than 23%, making Ireland second only to Belgium in the EU for the proportion of young adults with third-level degrees (OECD). Six out of ten of

Ireland's third-level students major in engineering, science or business studies. Coupled with a high level of proficiency in international languages, these achievements rank Ireland higher than its EU neighbours and the United States in the degree to which its education system meets the needs of a competitive economy (IMD). High educational standards have given people the vision, the knowledge and the competitive advantage to undertake enterprise initiatives and ultimately achieve a high level of success with them.

The significant 2001 slowdown in the United States, Eurozone and global economies and the global retrenchment of the information and communications industry will undoubtedly reduce economic growth rates in Ireland to more sustainable levels. These trends will be exacerbated by the serious negative impact on economic growth in the agribusiness and tourism sectors in Europe, including Ireland, arising from the most serious outbreak of foot-and-mouth disease for more than thirty years. Ireland is, however, immeasurably better able than in previous decades to survive these inevitable downswings in the international economy. That this is so is a tribute to the underlying competitiveness of the economy in terms of the industrial structure, the skills and educational attainment of the workforce, the strong public finance position of the government and the spirit of enterprise that has taken root in Irish society.

III
Irish enterprise spirit: Ability, imagination and passion

Statistics such as those detailed above give some insight into the transformation that has overtaken Irish society in the last decade. What they cannot do is describe the nature of the new spirit that has emerged. I have set out to capture that spirit by interviewing sixteen people who very clearly display an enterprising optimism and flair in their everyday actions and attitudes. The chapters that follow are fleeting pen portraits of these people. The objective is to describe how they have given practical expression to their enterprise talents, to understand why they have established their chosen enterprises, and to describe the influences that have driven them to succeed, the beliefs that underlie their commitment, and their perceptions of the changing environment in which they live and work. The stories are sometimes direct, casual and opinionated, but always refreshing, insightful and captivating.

All of the people in this collection share three striking characteristics, the combination of which makes perhaps for a distinctively Irish enterprise spirit: ability, imagination and passion. The ability of Chris Horn to apply highly complex research that facilitates computer networking has been invested in his enterprise, Iona Technologies. The imagination of Barry McDonagh in seeking new ways to generate a stronger sense of community in Ireland has led him to create a charity-focussed Internet site, thegoodspider.com. The passion of Brody Sweeney to overcome the financial and personal challenges of business failure has spurred him to create an Irish franchise brand, O'Brien's Irish Sandwich Bars, which enjoys worldwide recognition.

A *social capitalism?*
One last notable characteristic that distinguishes the Irish spirit of enterprise is an understated but strong and unyielding wish to give. Each of the enterprise leaders interviewed gives in many ways – much of their generosity going unrecorded. Whether devoting time and energy to education initiatives, funding

unrelated fledgling enterprises, building livelihoods, or participating in bringing the Special Olympics to Ireland for the first time, all have a strong sense that the benefits that accrue from enterprise should be shared. There is a common belief that individual achievements are set in a context of social progress and empathy with the needs of others.

The enterprise leaders in this book seem comfortable between the poles of a disciplined US economic model that promotes the invisible hand of development by way of unrestrained individual self-interest and the conscientious Northern European model that sets economic development within the context of a welfare state. While a government framework of regulation and law is essential in achieving the balance between individual and community interest, the ultimate determinant of that balance will be on the culture, beliefs and value systems of the individual members of a society. A society whose members have a strong sense of the value of both individual interest and community responsibility is one in which the quality of life of its citizens is higher and in which enterprise can thrive – a society, in fact, characterized by 'social capitalism'.

There is evidence in the following chapters of the emergence of such capitalism in Ireland, in which social responsibility plays a significant part. The challenge for Irish enterprise and for Irish society is to create a sustained balance between individual interest and community responsibility so that the quality of life for all Irish citizens can be further enhanced.

CHARLIE ARDAGH

Co-founder with brother, Rory, European Access

Providers; Former director, Formus Ireland;

Co-founder, First Tuesday Club Ireland

*C*harlie Ardagh is a serial entrepreneur. His spirit of enterprise is the epitome of what this book has set out to capture. He has graduated from selling vegetables in his neighbourhood to negotiating hundred-million-dollar financing deals. He has launched three telecommunications businesses in a period that witnessed high investor confidence give way to the ravages of the communications industry shakeout. In an effort to close the divide between young Irish entrepreneurs and the established investment community, he co-founded Ireland's First Tuesday Club, a monthly forum that incubates Irish companies of the future.

When I first met with Charlie in late 2000 to learn about his enterprise, we gazed out of his office at the International Financial Services Centre in Dublin and wondered at the social and economic changes that Ireland had experienced in recent years. We could only guess at what the future would bring. At that time, his parent company was on the verge of conducting an initial public offering that might value it at over $2 billion, making him a multimillionaire at the age of twenty-five. We could not have foreseen what the future would in fact unfold.

Bondi Beach, Australia, on hold

It does not seem long ago that I was finishing school and choosing which course to attend at college. I am neither very academic nor technically oriented, and my hopes of attending highbrow courses in Trinity College or University College Dublin did not work out. Instead, I went to a good college in Luton, England, and spent three years studying psychology and marketing. I enjoyed my studies, but Luton is a less than attractive city – I don't think anyone has ever thought to make a postcard of Luton. I finished my studies in June 1998. I had a big wad of plane tickets that I had received for my twenty-first birthday the previous December, and I had a great plan to fly around the world after graduation and spend some time with friends in Australia en route.

My brother, Rory, was in the middle of a master's degree in international management. He had started with two years of business, economics and social science at Trinity College and was continuing his studies with three sequential years in universities in Paris, Oxford and Berlin to achieve a Grand Diplôme des Ecoles d'Europe. Rory reads everything he can lay a hand to and soaks up information. He has a habit of building on this information to come up with ideas of great foresight. He churns out new concepts with an angle of understanding and perception that others might never imagine. While we were both in college, Rory and I struck up an e-mail dialogue about a whole series of different enterprise ideas. We would discuss such ideas as changes in the development of the Internet, electronic commerce, banking systems and technology.

In our e-mail banter we discussed one particular idea shared with us by a friend who worked at France Telecom. He had told us about a new technology emerging in the United States called 'wireless in the local loop' (WLL). The technology facilitated broadband data transmission via radio waves as opposed to fibre-optic cable, thus obviating the need to dig up streets in order to lay cable. He was sure it would be the next big wave of communications technology in Europe. We started doing some research and found out that licences to operate the WLL technology would soon become available in different European countries. Rory was very excited about the possibilities and really got the ball rolling in investigating the extent of the business opportunity. He looked into how the licences had been distributed and applied in the United States. He saw the value derived by those who had won licences and saw that the licences themselves were growing significantly in value over time. Although we did not fully understand the technology, we looked at the potential to capitalize on winning licences in Europe with a sense of opportunism. We looked upstream of the technology, from a regulatory perspective, and tried to figure out the first steps needed to carve some value from the advent of licensing.

The e-mails flew back and forth between Rory and me, and the more we explored the opportunity, the more interesting it became. We knew there was a pent-up demand for broadband and high-speed Internet access via radio waves. We understood that the capital requirement to start up a wireless network was limited because there was no need for civil engineering work to lay cables. We gathered information from engineering friends and contacts about what the technology meant. While the technology for the global system for mobile communications (GSM) was already mature, the WLL technology was at an earlier stage of development, which enabled brand-new start-ups to gain a foothold. We saw that companies such as Nortel, Cisco and Lucent were researching and prototyping the technology, so we felt that we could figure out the details of the technology when it was fully developed and make a leap of faith to apply for the licences in the meantime. We agreed to give the idea a shot and started to explore the mechanics of starting a company that would apply for European licences. At Easter of 1998, we set up a company called European Access Providers (EAP).

Rory had another year to complete in Berlin, but we knew that the opportunity was one we simply could not leave idle. I graduated in June, and conscious that all my friends were stretched out and sunning themselves on Bondi Beach in Australia, I cashed in my plane tickets and got to work. I finished college on a Friday, and by Monday morning I was busy.

Start-up

I began working in our family TV room at home. All I needed to get going was a computer with e-mail and a telephone. We secured £5,000 from the South Dublin County Enterprise Board. They required that we spend the £5,000 before they gave it to us, so we delved into savings accounts and got some support from home. Our only expenses were Internet and phone bills and some fact-finding journeys to companies in the United Kingdom. I lived on about £50 per fortnight. I engrossed myself in the details of the technology, the legalities of applying for licences and the competition directives of the European Union. I tried to learn as much as I could from the large, established companies in the United States, such as Winstar and Itelligent. I learnt a lot from their websites, as well as from simply ringing up and asking for information. I remember one time ringing from the TV room and saying, 'This is Charlie, the CEO of EAP', and getting through to the CEO of Winstar, which had 10,000 employees. Ironically, we would later compete on Belgian soil, where both Formus and Winstar won operating licences.

In the beginning, we had plans to apply for licences across Europe. This would have required significant funding. Unfortunately, when a 21-year-old who has never had a job enters a venture capital office, in a suit that is too small, looking for £200 million, the venture capital managers are not very receptive. They thought it was a great idea but were reluctant to invest in young unknowns. We decided to concentrate on Ireland and applied to the Office of the Director of Telecommunications Regulation (ODTR), under the directorship of Ms Etain Doyle, for a trial licence. The ODTR is the national regulatory authority for telecommunications in Ireland and was set up in 1997, when the telecom sector was changing rapidly as a result of deregulation activities. It is responsible for making the liberalized market work in accordance with both EU and Irish law and grants licences to companies to operate communications networks. It took long months of banging on the door to get a proper hearing from the ODTR. I believe that the basic issues concerning deregulation of telecommunications were higher on the agenda than a couple of young fellows looking for a trial licence for a new technology of which the ODTR had heard little. At first, we met with a little disbelief and questioning about what experience and backing we had. We were blinded by youthful enthusiasm. We did not realize that we should have been making hundred-million-dollar vendor financing deals. In retrospect, it was probably helpful not to have known the full extent of what we were getting ourselves into, because we were uninhibited. We had a vision of getting a licence, putting it to use and selling communications services. We were not thinking of every detail. Had we understood every detail, the prospect might have seemed less attractive and the vision would have been less clear. In fact, when we later hit teething problems in the implementation of the technology and found ourselves drawn into a swamp of technical detail, we would remind ourselves not to forget 'the vision'.

We spent days talking on the phone with the people at the ODTR, understanding what they required from us and trying to convince them that we would put what we agreed was a national resource to good use. By Christmas of 1998, I began to feel frustrated. We were getting no love from the ODTR. Every week they would have ten questions for us. Every week we sat down and answered the questions in such a way that we felt they could not possibly have any room for more questions. Every week they came back with ten more. We tried to believe that we were only ever ten questions away from being allowed to get the business up and running, but at times I felt disheartened enough to want to get on a plane to New York and start over again. However, Rory and I really believed that we could make the business work. We knew there would be a demand, and the numbers in our business plan were enough to keep our motivation up. Most of all, my trust in Rory, the source of the idea, did not diminish.

To our great relief, our efforts and persistence eventually paid off, and EAP was granted a trial licence. This was crucial because it gave us a first-mover advantage. A company that acts first on a new technology and is the first to bring it to market earns value through a natural association with the technology. At last we had the credibility we needed with this licence. We had carved a niche for ourselves in Ireland with a reputation as people who knew a lot about the technology, were well known to the Regulator and had the enthusiasm required to see implementation through to completion.

We secured some seed venture capital and went in search of a partner. While Rory continued his studies in Berlin, I did the graveyard shift on the telephone all night to prospective partners in the United States. A company called Formus Communications, based in Denver, had a lot of good knowledge and expertise in the WLL technology, had serious venture capital backing and was turning its attention to Europe. It seemed like an ideal fit.

I brought Formus representatives to Dublin to whet their appetite for a partnership with us. I invited a lawyer acquaintance to join me, and we sat down with Formus, engaged with them, did a horse trade and struck a deal. In effect, we created a joint venture, Formus Communications Ireland, of which EAP owned 20%. We brought our local credibility and knowledge, and they contributed the technical know-how and funding. Rory and I became directors of the company and were joined by Terri McNulty of Formus Communications, as chief executive officer. Terri was a terrific CEO. Rory, Terri and I learnt a lot from each other through out the start-up period of searching for offices and revising the business plans.

Licence to operate

The next step for our new company was to apply for a full wireless local loop licence. We set up teams in Dublin, Stockholm, Denver and Durban, and each contributed a different element to our bid application. The closer we got to the bid submission deadline, the harder we worked. Eventually, the Dublin team worked around the clock. For days on end, I would leave the office at 5 a.m., shower, shave, get some air and be back in the office, working on the bid, at 7 a.m.

On 6 May 1999, we duly submitted our application at midday, two hours before the deadline. There was a tremendous atmosphere of collective relief as competing bid teams converged at the Regulator's Office. The relentless hard work in preparing the bid and arranging the huge amount of paperwork, as well as the prospect of no sleep, was all over. We went for a lunchtime sandwich and a beer, and all nodded off in our suits. We had driven ourselves through the process with adrenaline and charged energy, but once it was over and I got home, I slept for days.

We were elated when it was announced in September that we had been awarded one of four licences, along with Esat, Eircell and Princes Holdings, the last being a venture 50% owned by Tony O'Reilly's Independent Group. A protracted court battle ensued as Broadnet contested the rejection of their bid, and we were not granted an official licence until ten months later, in June 2000. In the meantime, Terri, Rory and I started hiring people and putting business processes in place. This was a major risk, as we were burning money in advance of official confirmation that we had won the licence, but we believed it would give us the advantage of stealing a march on the competition.

We started to build an infrastructure that cost $60 million and consisted of a series of shoebox-sized antennae and accompanying control equipment, placed strategically on masts across the country. We had an overheads burn rate of some $1 million per month. These high investment costs were necessary for the growth phase of the business and would be followed by a positive cash flow some four years later, as laid out in our business plan. We negotiated with Deutsche

Bank to provide the necessary funds and with Lucent Technologies, who were to build our network, to guarantee the loan. Prior to our official launch in November 2000, we had already enlisted over twenty corporate customers. We built a workforce of some eighty-five people and set up offices in the International Financial Services Centre district. The mix of engineering, sales, marketing and finance people made for a healthy and diverse work environment. The atmosphere was great. People liked their work, and they liked working for a growing company with an exciting future. Every employee owned a stake in the company, and that was a big incentive to work hard. While we did not have the standard basketball court or pool tables of a new-economy company, there was a real sense that Formus was a fun place to work. We created a relaxed, open and accessible atmosphere. We had a flat organizational structure with no intentional hierarchy, and everyone was called by their first name. An auditor once confused several of us by referring to our financial director, Brian, as Mr Murphy. Formus was a home and a future.

Collapse and rebuilding

Out of the blue, on 13 March 2001, the plug was pulled. Terri had been on a break in Spain and received a call insisting that she fly directly to a company meeting in Munich. I took a call from Terri, and she broke the news that Formus was shutting down operations in Ireland. I was stunned and devastated. Everything had been going so well – we had won the licence to operate, were building the necessary infrastructure and had signed up customers – and now the mother company was deserting us. The exchange that Rory and I had is unprintable. We gathered the facts from Terri to try to understand why events had taken this sudden change of course. Formus Communications had been having serious cash-flow difficulties unknown to us. The company had stakes in several European locations besides Ireland and was laying out huge cash amounts to build the required infrastructure. The only indication of difficulty we had been given was a note in late 2000 explaining that we should maintain expenditures within our agreed budgets. Formus Communications had planned an imminent IPO and was in discussions with strategic partners. We believed that both of these activities would secure a healthy cash flow for the company. However, in March, the banking institutions that had provided bridging loans to Formus started to become worried about delays in conducting an IPO and were nervous about the deteriorating telecommunications environment. They held a crisis meeting in the United States and insisted that Formus close its operations in Norway, Sweden, Denmark, Finland and Ireland. As financers, the bankers had ultimate power. In despair, the closures were agreed, and the chairman of Formus resigned.

The afternoon that we heard the news from Terri, we gathered all our staff together and told them what was going on. We explained that we had one week to find a partner to replace Formus before being forced into liquidation. They were terribly downhearted but were united in their hopes that we would find a partner. We set up a crisis team with Rory, myself, Terri, Brian Murphy, our financial director, David Parkinson, our technical director, John Sharp, our sales manager, and Kevin Dunphy, our operations manager. Our equipment supplier, Lucent, insisted that a partner should provide a huge guarantee of $50 million. For a full week, we banged on doors to generate a spark of interest in potential partners. Every day we held a 4 p.m. meeting with the staff to update them on progress. We just did not have enough time to save the company, and one week after the news had first broken, it was all over. A liquidator was appointed, and we closed the doors for the last time. There was a dramatic sense of loss. We had gone from enjoying a tremendous daily atmosphere at work to absolutely nothing. It was very sad.

Nobody goes out of business on purpose. Our staff, who had lost their jobs, and our creditors, who were owed $20 million, knew that. A week after we closed, we held a party to raise funds for a colleague's unwell child, and three-quarters of the former staff turned out. There was no bitterness or sense of failure. They agree that the experience makes them stronger for the future. I learnt three good lessons from the collapse of Formus Ireland. Firstly, it is crucial to have full transparency regarding the financial health of a partner. We should have insisted on seeing where the money was flowing. Secondly, we became too dependent on our partner and worked at a distance, such that we had no direct impact on central decisions. There was nothing Rory or I could do about the decision to abandon Formus Ireland. Lastly, I will ensure that my next company will have the same level of commitment from staff as I experienced in Formus. The atmosphere was so positive and was based on the belief that work should be less about graft and more about being a party of life.

In the week that we searched for a partner, Rory and I started to cook some new ideas. We knew we had done nothing wrong in principle with Formus Ireland but that the rough telecommunications environment and central cash-flow problems had caused the downfall. We knew the business well, had excellent contacts and had won respect and credibility. We decided we were not going to go away. We have since started a new telecommunications company that is going through an early moulding phase. We are courting investor interest and building resources. We hope to attract many of the people that worked with us in Formus. With an upcoming official launch, these are exciting days. Despite the comfortable office and perks that I enjoyed at Formus, I have always preferred the dealing involved in creating a new business. In that way, I am doing what I enjoy most again, but this time I carry a wealth of experience.

Brothers and family

Rory and I complement each other very well. Rory is an excellent technical person and is a self-taught information technology expert. Selling an idea, securing partners and raising money is all about talk, which is where my marketing skills are useful. In fact, while we each have strong skills in our own disciplines, we are both all-rounders. We could not have launched our businesses successfully without both of us having a good understanding of business planning and finance. We could not maintain our business successfully without a good understanding of our customers and their needs. We combine to create something even stronger than the sum of the individuals. When we get together, it is a case of one plus one is three. We each have achieved what we have only with the help of the other. At the outset, we needed each other to launch EAP. I would not have been involved were it not for Rory's initial idea and his knowledge of the technology and licensing activities in the United States, and Rory would not have got the company up and running because he was still studying in Berlin at the time. We do have our heated moments and have impassioned arguments about some issues. We are brothers, after all, but we have always trusted and respected each other.

When Rory and I were young, we ran a series of small enterprise activities. Along with some friends, Rory and I would go from door to door on our estate and take orders from all the neighbours for potatoes and vegetables. Then we would get our father to drive us into Moore Street to pick up the orders, and we would sell them at a profit. We also tried our hand at running a few discos in city clubs. The discos were mainly for our school friends, because I was a school captain and I enjoyed organizing entertainment and social events. I always had a special interest in entertainment. In fact, if I had not become so involved in business activities as a first choice, I would have liked to try my hand at acting.

I have never followed my acting inclination seriously, although I often put myself in the shoes of customers and walk around a little to try to imagine their point of view and what their needs are. The idea of working in business had a great personal attraction for me in not having to work for somebody else. My father and each of his brothers, as well as their father, all worked for themselves, so I am sure an independent characteristic runs in the family. The support of our family certainly made it easier for Rory and me to launch into business. My parents would say, 'Charlie is taking a year off after college. He has a great degree that any employer could use, or he could be travelling the world, but instead he has teamed up with Rory and is sitting in our TV room getting a company off the ground, and we are very proud of both of them.' While they did not become involved in the details of the business at any time, our parents' support was very important and helpful to us. There were days when I would have little or nothing to do. I would be waiting for calls to come through or anticipating an e-mail from the ODTR, knowing that if we did not get a trial licence, all our efforts and sweat would have been wasted. On days like this, the encouragement from people close to us carried us through.

Youth on our side

Youth is on our side. Bankers and venture capital investors have not always agreed. Rory and I have been frustrated to face puzzled looks and ignorance of the potential of the technology when banging on doors for funding. At the moment of walking into a meeting, armed with a business plan, we could read in a venture capital manager's eyes that he or she wished we were twenty years older and had more experience in what we were trying to do. We started bringing older legal representatives with us simply to have a few more grey hairs in the room. They did not know much about the technology, but they learnt as we went along. The credibility and perception of professionalism that they added by virtue of their age engendered a greater willingness to listen in the managers we visited.

Between May and September 1999, while we were waiting for an answer to our bid submission for an operating licence for Formus, we spent much time wondering how to overcome the youth credibility issue. This was the zenith of the e-revolution, when the Nasdaq was hitting dizzying heights, fifteen-year-old kids with bright ideas were getting money thrown at them in Silicon Valley, and high-tech companies floating for $1 a share one day were worth $400 a share the next. Investment in young people and their ideas was intense in the United States, and we wanted to recreate some of this in Ireland. We decided to run informal events at which young Irish people with enterprising ideas could meet investors and chat casually about their ideas. The advantage would be twofold. Firstly, young entrepreneurs would be able to meet investors, pitch their ideas and get valuable feedback and advice. Secondly, investors would get first-hand access to budding entrepreneurs and overcome the constraints of formality that might otherwise smother their ability to appreciate a good idea when they saw it. We wanted to create a shift of culture in Ireland. We wanted investors to overcome the established traditions of stuffy investment review meetings and meet young, enterprising people in a less forbidding environment. They would be far better able to understand problems that young people face, such as lack of experience and finance, yet still recognize ideas that could be the next big Irish enterprise success story. We hoped that the exchange of ideas would be much less intimidating and would result in an acceleration of investment and start-up of new enterprises.

First Tuesday Club

The idea was similar to a new incubator concept, called the First Tuesday Club, which had started in London a year earlier. Today there are First Tuesday Clubs in more than 100 cities, with a membership of more than 100,000 – a tremendously valuable database and network facility. We met other young people in Dublin who shared the idea, one of whom rang the London First Tuesday Club organizers, explained what we were going to do and asked if we could call ourselves 'First Tuesday Club Ireland'. Along with founders David Neville and Marc Butterly, we arranged our inaugural First Tuesday Club session in September 1999, in a Dublin city-centre bar called Zanzibar. We organized for guest speakers from the established business community to address the session attendees. We also gave people the opportunity to make 'elevator pitches' from a podium. Imagine you have an enterprising idea, and you get into a lift beside a major investment manager on the ground floor. What do you pitch at him in the three minutes you have before he gets off on the twentieth floor?

The first session we ran was very cool and punchy. We thought we might only get thirty or forty people to turn up at Zanzibar. I remember Rory and I driving down O'Connell Street to get to the venue. We had a great big 'First Tuesday' sign that was so long that Rory had to hang out the window of my Dad's car to hold on to it, while I drove. I think the sign is still in Zanzibar, in fact. From the car we could see suits coming from every direction of the city, converging on the First Tuesday Club. There was a tremendous buzz, and we were overwhelmed with the 250 people who packed the venue to capacity. Entrepreneur Colm Grealy addressed the audience with a message to 'open your minds to enterprise and "be original"'. Colm is the founder and CEO of Online.ie and also started the company Ireland On-Line with associate Barry Flanagan. They later sold it to PostGEM, and PostGEM/IOL was ultimately sold to Esat for £115 million.

I am no longer involved in First Tuesday events, although the club continues to thrive under the excellent direction of David Neville and Marc Butterly, with the co-ordination of Jackie Garvey of Enterprise Ireland. The constituency of First Tuesday Ireland has expanded to include more than 6,000 enterprise leaders. Events are so popular that they are often oversubscribed, with the result that even members have to apply to attend events.

First Tuesday's popularity is a reflection of a bubbling enterprise culture in Ireland. You will always find a great diversity of characters attending. There will be technology experts, humble entrepreneurs learning how to pitch, venture capital managers looking for the next big dotcom company, journalists searching for a story and lawyers offering advice for equity. There is a vibrant atmosphere that I believe is a new phenomenon. Apparently, the 1980s were dull by comparison.

These days, young people assume the confidence to 'have a go' at a new venture. I have many friends throwing their energy into enterprising ideas. One has started a vending-machine company. Another rents DJs to parties and entertainment events – all it took was some contacts and an advertisement in the *Golden Pages*, and he is taking a royalty from guys driving around with a bunch of CDs. This enterprise activity is only to be expected in a country where 50% of the population are under the age of twenty-eight – they have to do something for a living, and surplus cash is in circulation, waiting to be harnessed. The annual Young Scientists' Exhibition is a wonderful example of youth enterprise. The projects on display and the work invested in their creation show remarkable innovation. Every year, hundreds of projects demonstrate everyday applications in an enterprising way. The exhibition is a showcase for the inventiveness of young Irish people.

Throughout the country, people demonstrate enterprise ability and inventiveness. These attributes are founded on confidence and the audacity to push the established limits. I feel that young Irish people have been growing in confidence in recent years. There is a great new sense of self-belief. Finding employment is no longer a struggle, and self-employment is becoming a path of choice. Irish people have always left a positive mark in countries to which they have travelled. Now more than ever, they are proving their ability at home.

In control

I love what I do. I could never work under the thumb of a boss. I would rather work on the next revolution in pencil-parers than work a nine-to-five job. Because I am an agreeable chap, I might well have started in a regular job, but I would not have lasted long. I am unorganized and unpunctual. I would not survive in a normal environment. I need to set my own personal goals, which are always stretching higher and farther away and which keep me motivated. I am always asking questions of my ability and trying to push my own limits. I have been on a 45-degree learning curve for the last three years, and there is no sign of slowing down. When the curve drops, I know I will find something else for stimulation. Over the three years, the motivation has become less about making a buck and more about the buzz I feel from what I am learning. I get a great kick out of thinking how much I have learnt since the days I worked out of the TV room. The downside in any business enterprise is the risk associated with launching a new venture and the months and months of unpaid effort. I have absolutely no regrets when I think about Formus. Being a paper millionaire will not mean a lot to me again. I approach every new deal with a straight face and a tough mindset now, but I am stronger for the experience, and I enjoy what I do immensely. Some people get a job with a steady income, settle in their minds and go to their local bar to meet friends twice a week. Some people like that – not I. I prefer the energy and the fun of enterprise. It has given me what I greatly value – I am in control of my own life.

MOYA DOHERTY

Television producer; Founder and director,
Tyrone Productions; Creator of Riverdance

*A*t Moya Doherty's office on Little Mary Street in Dublin's
city centre, many worlds meet. Two overwhelming aged
stone monuments guard the inner entrance, contrasting vividly
with the modern interior, with its glass elevator. An abundance
of stone, glass and wood gives the enclosed space a sense of the
outdoors. In her career, Moya Doherty has shown a similar
flair for reconciling seeming opposites. She has combined
business and artistic creativity in the management of her
company, Tyrone Productions. Her television productions have
blended imagination and reality. She has fused traditional Irish
culture and modern spectacle in her most memorable creation,
Riverdance, *the success of which has transcended geographical*
and cultural diversity by bringing international audiences to
their feet.

The Riverdance *phenomenon has emerged at a time when*
Irish cultural identity is growing in confidence. Economic
prosperity and the prospect of peace in Northern Ireland have
had a liberating effect. These developments have created the
space to reflect on Irish culture and appreciate it in a positive
and constructive way. The enterprise of Moya Doherty and her
husband, John Colgan, has not only ensured the success of
Riverdance *but has also undoubtedly acted as a catalyst to this*
fresh reflection. Their vision has helped to transform

traditional Irish dancing and music into an internationally popular expression of contemporary Irish culture that has enchanted tens of millions of people throughout the world.

Childhood memories

When I was a child in Donegal, I had a great relationship with a black cat. The cat and I would go on fantasy journeys for days and weeks. We would have wonderful adventures together. Just as many children at times feel lonely and isolated and need to communicate this in some way, I found great solace in my black cat. My parents, both schoolteachers, decided that we should move to Dublin just after my First Communion. I remember that every summer I would climb onto blankets in the back of our Austin Cambridge and travel back to Donegal to stay with different cousins. I have memories of long days on the beach when the summers seemed to be warmer and longer and my sandals stuck to the tar on the road and I seemed to be eating ice cream every day – it was lovely.

My reaction to my schooldays is mixed, but I was comfortable with my studies. I was sometimes rebellious and anarchic. I felt uncomfortable in a system that was too structured, and I did not like authoritarian figures. I think this had something to do with being the child of schoolteachers. One of the yardsticks by which we were measured at home was academic achievement. The rest of my family went on to study forever – I have two older sisters and two younger brothers. I opted out. When I look back, I feel lucky to have met two teachers who really inspired me. The first was Ms O'Regan in Belgrove National School, Clontarf, who introduced me to the wealth of poetry. She was a wonderful woman from Galway who has passed away since. Ms O'Regan would make us stand on top of our chairs and recite our favourite poems. This opened up a whole new world of fantasy to me and removed any inhibitions about performing to an audience. In my secondary school, Manor House, Raheny, I met another wonderful teacher who left a deep and positive impact – Una Parker. Ms Parker taught me drama and sparked a flame of interest that was waiting to be lit. Throughout my secondary school years, my only ambition was to act. I was utterly and completely passionate about it.

Shattered illusions

When I left school in the mid-1970s, I considered studying Irish and French in university, but the appeal was not strong enough to distract me from following my passion to become an actor. At that time, acting was a difficult profession to breach in Ireland, and travelling to England to join an acting troupe was something I could not financially afford to do. I decided to take a secretarial course and subsequently got a job as a secretary in RTÉ. I intended to get involved in the drama department at RTÉ or perhaps join the Raidió Éireann Players acting group. Like many an 'aspiring actor', I was biding time before I got the break I needed.

I had worked with RTÉ for only a year when I gained an acting position with the Team Educational Theatre Company. I was delighted with this opportunity and happily went touring with them for a year. I very soon realized that although I loved acting, it was not to be my career for life. My time with Team left me with many great friends and a huge respect for the hard work that actors invest and the resilience they must have in order to deal with the audition rejections they often suffer.

I returned to RTÉ as a production assistant – work that was

challenging and satisfying. I worked on a great variety of programmes, including entertainment, drama and features. I was assigned to work with a particular producer or director and worked closely with them in developing a production. I loved working under pressure, having a sense of order and getting things to work out right and on time. This was a tremendous training for me. The time commitment that my work demanded was so great that I could not maintain even fringe involvement in theatre, unfortunately, although I did run a drama group for the staff for a short while. I met John, my husband, in RTÉ at this time, when I worked as a production assistant to him for a year.

While I was not overtly ambitious, I did apply for promotion opportunities when they arose. I moved very quickly through different grades within RTÉ. It was a time in the early 1980s when a depressing atmosphere was descending on Ireland. There was a social backdrop of the anti-divorce and anti-abortion campaigns and high unemployment. It was an unusual and uncomfortable time in the development of our state and our culture. John decided he wanted to get out and go to Britain. I was happy to leave also, and I resigned my job as a production assistant. After I handed in my resignation, Anne McCabe, an RTÉ producer, approached me and asked if I would present an arts programme on television called The Live Arts. I knew this was a great opportunity, and despite my desire to leave with John, I remained in Dublin and presented the programme for a year. With good presenting experience, I was ready for another move and flew to London.

London and identity

Travelling abroad to London was one of the most worthwhile things I ever did because it gave me great independence and a great sense of self. As an Irish person living in a different country, I had to come to terms with an identity that was under constant challenge. The frequent bombings in England created a very uncomfortable atmosphere for the Irish. Working in England also instilled an appreciation of and strong connection with the challenges that my grandparents might have faced when they emigrated for a period to England and America to make a living.

I worked for five years as a reporter and a producer with TV AM. After some time I started to become less comfortable with presenting, as I felt I was not very well suited to being the front person. There were plenty of presenting opportunities to pursue, and while I enjoyed presenting, I decided once again that this was something that could not be a life career. I became more attracted to the concept of producing and I applied for a producer/director's job back at RTÉ.

Even though I remember one particular friend writing to me and asking me if I was crazy in thinking to return, I was ready to come home. At the age of twenty-nine, I came back to Dublin and joined a production-training course in RTÉ. Journalist Michael Heney ran the course, which proved to be a tremendous learning experience. I met some hugely talented people from whom I learnt a great deal, including friends and colleagues Ann Enright, Kevin Linehan, Hillary Orpen and Charlie McCarthy. The stimulating environment on the course challenged us to deliver very creative and innovative material.

Television production

I embarked on a new phase of my life as a TV producer. It proved to be one of the most challenging and creatively satisfying periods of my career to date. Despite this fulfilment I have learnt that I certainly am a restless person, always seeking a new challenge as soon as I have achieved a level of comfort with my current activity.

RTÉ's *People in Need Telethon* was my first television production and a hugely exciting project. My next production was *The Silent Scream* – a documentary on child sexual abuse in Ireland. While both of these projects were very demanding and very different, they were equally challenging and rewarding.

Clear vision is the most important attribute a producer can have. The ability to communicate that vision to a production team without allowing it to be diluted is also crucial. Understanding exactly the message, tone and atmosphere you wish to convey, and ensuring that a well-organized team is aligned with these provides the basis for a high-quality production. I try to invest most thinking and planning in the early stages of a production. Advance strategy and contingency planning eliminate the disorganized chaos that can descend on an artistic project when it is under way. I prefer to approach a production very well prepared and then devote my energy to its execution. However, it is important to have an open mind and take on board creative input from other members of the team.

With solid experience in making programmes both in Ireland and in the United Kingdom, John and I decided to launch our own independent production company, Tyrone Productions, in 1987. It was exciting to launch an enterprise, and most importantly, it gave John and me a new freedom in production and creative thinking. Owning and directing our own production company gave us the space to control our own time, ideas and energy.

Tyrone Productions has grown to become the biggest independent production company in Ireland. John and I are directors of Tyrone Productions, but it is has been managing director Joan Egan who has developed Tyrone Productions and achieved successes that none of us could have imagined. Tyrone's productions include *Open House, Wanderlust, School Around the Corner, Ros na Rún* and, most recently, the Irish version of *Who Wants to Be a Millionaire?*

The 1994 Eurovision Song Contest

In 1994 RTÉ's director of programming at the time, Liam Miller, asked me to produce the *Eurovision Song Contest*. At first, I was not at all keen on the idea, because I had just finished the annual *People in Need Telethon* and had two small boys who needed more attention. I needed some time out and was reluctant to take it. However, the more I considered the idea, the more intrigued I became, not with the entire *Eurovision* show, but rather with the potential of the interval act. While the main body of the show itself left little room for originality, the interval act was something of a carte blanche for creativity. It was an exciting opportunity to showcase unique Irish talent and culture to over 600 million people throughout the world in a way they had never experienced. I went back to Liam and agreed to be the executive producer.

I decided to commission the creation of a performance from a contemporary Irish composer that would showcase the best of Irish music and dance. I did not want an act rooted in the past but one that projected Ireland's exciting present. Ireland of the mid-1990s was a place of great enthusiasm and hope, and it stirred with a pounding spirit of development. I wanted the core of the act to be a vibrant, sexy, contemporary Irish tap-dance routine, starring two lead dancers supported by a backing troupe. This is how I laid out the interval act, on a single sheet of white paper.

My next step was to transform the two-dimensional idea into a three-dimensional reality. That very year, John had produced a show for television in the National Concert Hall that celebrated five millennia of culture in Co. Mayo. The concert featured two Irish-American dancers, Jean Butler from Long Island and Michael Flatley from Chicago. Michael performed a solo dance, and Jean performed with her dance partner, Colin Dunne. Michael's dance was a mix of Latin and Irish passion with influences of flamenco, tap and traditional Irish dance. Jean was beautiful, and her dancing was stunningly natural. I knew that if they were cast to dance together, it would be spectacular.

I phoned Michael at his home in Beverly Hills and persuaded him to dance for us. Jean was harder to track down, as she was on tour in Japan with the Chieftains, but when I reached her at last, she also agreed to appear in the interval. My next and very important phone call was to the composer of the Mayo concert, Bill Whelan, and he was very happy to work on the *Eurovision* interval act. I contacted an old friend of mine, Mavis Ascott, and asked her to be the choreographer.

Along with the interval act, I was absorbed in a lot of other organizational tasks for the production of the *Eurovision*. I fought very hard to change the voting system from what I believed to be an antiquated system of telephone voting to a more modern television voting system, with pictures from all the participating countries broadcast live via satellite. I ran into trouble with this proposed change. I did not have the support of the international managers of the European Broadcasting Union (EBU). While RTÉ was very supportive, some of the 'old guard' in the EBU did not like the idea of pushing the boundaries and scrapping the telephone voting system. I was told that participating countries would be contacted to see if they agreed. Days later, I was told that the proposal had been investigated and that I did not have the support required. I was baffled that others would not support the removal of such an archaic system. I felt that the EBU simply did not want to make the change because it did not suit them and decided to gauge the level of international support myself. Together with production co-ordinator, Marie Travers, I worked late into the night in my office and contacted every one of the participating countries by fax, outlining the reasoning and proposal for the voting changes and asking for their support. This was a contest within a contest. The following day, the faxes started to arrive one after the other. Each said, 'Yes, we will support you.' I had a wonderful feeling of justification. By the end of the day, we had all the support needed.

The lesson I learnt from this episode was not to take no for an answer. If somebody tells me that something cannot be done, I want to find a way. I ask why not rather than why. There are numerous ways to fulfil an idea. If I meet a brick wall on one path, I will return to the start and find another path and carry the idea in a different direction.

Riverdance

The more we developed the interval act, the more I knew we had something quite extraordinary and special, something very powerful and dramatic. I was also aware that it was only six minutes and forty seconds of a three-hour programme, and as the night approached I became absorbed in other operational aspects of the show for which I was responsible from beginning to end.

I had seen the interval act many times during rehearsals but never in front of a live audience. On the big night itself, I was so busy ensuring the quality reception of the satellite pictures from all over Europe that I did not even get to see the interval act live. I was sitting in the back room with the head of sound operations, Charlie Byrne, and other members of the team who were working on the satellite pictures, and they said, 'They are on their feet', and I said, 'Who's on their feet?' With a sense of amazement, Charlie said, 'The audience, the audience are on their feet.' I leapt up, stuck my head out of the operations room and savoured the moment for about thirty seconds and then returned to call Slovakia. It was an extraordinary moment. It was on that night, 30 April 1994, that *Riverdance* was born.

Ireland also won the *Eurovision Song Contest* that year. The show had been an entire success for director Patrick Conway, myself and the entire team, but when it was all over, I was exhausted. I was so tired, in fact, that I could not sleep for a week, as my sleep pattern had been completely thrown out. I had been going to bed in the early hours and getting up at dawn to work extremely hard. In the aftermath, I remember pacing around the house with a lot of nervous energy. All I wanted to do was to go away with my family. We went on a camping holiday to France. When we returned, the initial positive support for the interval act had swelled to a phenomenal scale.

Liam Miller approached me and asked if I would produce a one-hour television special based on the *Riverdance* act. My gut reaction was that it would be a great idea, but after some thought I realized that part of the magic of *Riverdance* was in the passionate reaction it inspired in a live audience and concluded that we should produce a major live stage production that could be televised. I sat down with Bill Whelan and my husband, John, and we discussed how we might shape the stage show and seek development money. Then we took a bold step and booked the enormous Point Theatre in Dublin. That was the moment that we realized we had a major project on our hands and a real goal to work towards, with only our combined creativity and enterprise to help us. We booked the Point for an opening night on 9 February 1995. I originally wanted to have the show ready by Christmas, but that proved simply too ambitious. We could not afford any great delays because if we did not open the show before the following *Eurovision*, to be hosted by Ireland in April, the opportunity to exploit the sensation of *Riverdance* would have effectively passed.

To the Point

In staging *Riverdance* we had undertaken a serious business project. The upsides would be rewarding and fulfilling, but the downsides were equally uninviting. I worked, with great support from Joan Egan, in approaching investors, securing finance and putting a support package together. Dealing with the financial and investment side of the show was new to me. I enjoyed it a lot. Initial investment amounted to £1.3 million, more funds than I had ever managed up to that time. Managing the budget of our own enterprise initiative was daunting because we did not have the legal and accounting resources in the outside world that were available to a producer in RTÉ.

We raised £400,000 for the first show from a series of separate investors. These included Paul McGuinness, manager of U2; RTÉ Enterprises; Harry Crosbie, a Dublin property developer; Maurice Cassidy, a Dublin-based entertainment promoter; and an associate of Maurice's, Tommy Higgins. We received a very important injection of £100,000 in sponsorship from AIB. John and I staked our home and savings against the balance and took an enormous personal risk in the process. We calculated that we needed to sell 40% of the available 3,500 tickets for each of the performances over five weeks to cover our personal risk. The overall break-even point without profits would be met by selling 70% of all seats. It was quite a heavy mental burden. I am usually so cautious I would not bet on a horse. I remember driving home along the Dublin docks with John after a particularly tense day and feeling very fearful for our future, with so many uncertainties. John turned with a confident look and reassured me that it was going to work out. That was all I needed to hear.

Thankfully, the box office opened to record-breaking ticket sales. The entire five-week run sold out before the show had opened. We could breathe easily again and enjoy the final rehearsals. It was wonderful to meet Russian dancers, flamenco dancers, gospel choirs and all sorts of extraordinary musicians at Dublin Airport as they arrived in January for rehearsals at the Point.

I remember somebody telling me on the opening night at the Point that 'this is as good as it gets'. Thrilling as it was, it actually did get better – it became extraordinary. We developed and improved the show. Bill, John and I knew that we could take the show on the road. More than 600 million people had got a taste for *Riverdance*, and promoters from the United Kingdom, Germany and Australia were calling us trying to book performances abroad. The three of us wanted to develop the show further. We wanted more time and money to create the greatest Irish show that would play in front of massive audiences across the world. We spent a year and a half refining *Riverdance* and invested in it a lot of passion and love.

A *family of performers*

There is no doubt that the pairing of Jean Butler and Michael Flatley, along with composer Bill Whelan, proved to be an extraordinary team. The American influences on Irish dance brought a fresh perspective to our traditional ideas. Most of the support team who joined us at the outset have stayed with *Riverdance* through the years. We chose Irish costume designers, lighting designers and set designers. We have all generated close and strong relationships and will continue to work together. Julian Erskine has taken on the role of executive producer, and Maurice Cassidy is our international consultant. Maurice has become the strategic thinker who guides the international promotion and growth of *Riverdance*. These top managers have afforded me the ability to pull back and enjoy the business from a co-ordinating position.

Early in the life of *Riverdance*, we contracted performers show by show. Dancers and musicians would sign for a four-week run in London, for example. It is a testament to teamwork and enjoyment of the show that almost all of the original cast have stayed with the show and secured long-term contracts, with one notable exception. I believe that we made the right decision for *Riverdance* and ultimately the right decision for Michael Flatley in not renewing his contract as principal dancer. His tumultuous exit taught me a worthwhile lesson about being in the jaws of the media. So much press coverage about the departure of Michael was fundamentally untrue that I found the best response was to say nothing and let the issue play itself out. The inaccurate reporting and the spotlight of attention was hard to take. After some time, the media lost interest and the dust settled. In retrospect, the decision for Michael and *Riverdance* to part ways was the best thing for the continued success of *Riverdance*. Michael needed to create a different, Las Vegas, type of show, and to his credit, he did very well, but it was not the vision that we had for *Riverdance*.

It is difficult for performers to handle overnight success. The life of a performer is an extremely difficult one. We have so many extraordinarily talented people in our show who perform to their limits night after night, travelling to every corner of the world and giving up their hearts to every audience. It is wonderfully exhilarating but also exhaustingly demanding.

The show goes on

When we arrived in New York to perform at its most acclaimed venue, the 6,000-seat Radio City Music Hall, our dancers found that the stage was too hard to dance on. It was like steel and had no spring. Our dancers need to pound on a stage that springs with them and does not cause damage to their joints. This was a very serious problem because, for the first time, we faced the possibility that the show could not go on. We realized that Irish dancers do not come from a tradition of warming up, and so we hired numerous masseuses and physiotherapists to work with them. We could not take the stiffness out of the floor, so we took it out of the dancers. We also agreed never to arrive at a venue again and find ourselves in the same situation, and we now transport our own floors as part of an overall set designed by Robert Ballagh to every concert venue.

Over 10 million people have seen *Riverdance* worldwide. We have three *Riverdance* shows travelling around the world at the same time. One is stationed on Broadway and called The Shannon. Another, The Lagan, tours North America and packs 2,000-seat theatres every night. The third, The Liffey, is the production that played in Ireland in 2000 and travels throughout Europe, Asia and Australia.

Riverdance has been a very fast-moving juggernaut for me. When I took the wheel at the outset, it was demanding and challenging. Managing it as a business and keeping it on track set me on a steep learning curve because its momentum and speed were so great. We all learnt as we went along and created the template anew every day. Sometimes it was hard to maintain an overview, and sometimes we made mistakes, but there is not much I would change given the chance.

Homecoming

Riverdance grew out of a period of optimism in Ireland. At the threshold of an economic boom we are still riding, people were beginning to feel more optimistic about being Irish and more comfortable about Irish culture. *Riverdance* was an integral part of people's changing attitudes in terms of feeling positive about Irish culture and grasping a new sense of what it meant to be Irish. *Riverdance* may in fact have been a step ahead of these changing attitudes or travelled hand in hand with them. Who knows?

Six years after its creation, *Riverdance* is still extraordinary. I feared that the huge hype and the media coverage of Michael Flatley's exit had left Irish people sick and tired of hearing about the show. In the summer of 2000, we returned to the Point Theatre in Dublin with a show that had been refined to excellence compared to its debut run in the same theatre. The show played a smashing sell-out run. Returning to such a welcoming and warm Irish audience was a real homecoming and I think, for me, was the absolute highlight of the six years of *Riverdance*.

I will cherish and value the memories of *Riverdance* when I am old and grey and sitting in my rocking-chair. In fairness, I was in the right place, at the right time. I had the bones of a good idea, and a team of people came together and put flesh on it. It is extraordinary for all of us to have achieved the success we have enjoyed – it is a very good feeling.

Tyrone Productions has produced two *Riverdance* shows on video, as well as a *Riverdance* documentary. The sales of these videos have been phenomenal: 125,000 units have been sold in Ireland, 150,000 in Germany, 350,000 in Australia and New Zealand, 2.2 million in the United Kingdom, 3 million in the United States and tens of thousands more across Europe, Latin America and South Africa. The combined sales amounted to over $70 million – a guarantee for the future of Tyrone Productions. Tyrone Productions remains an active and exciting production house. Independent companies like Tyrone have made positive changes to the Irish production industry. Companies are not thinking in local terms as they did in the past. New productions not only target the Irish market but have international saleability and appeal.

Husband and wife, business and creativity

John and I have been together for almost twenty years. We have worked together in many different capacities throughout those years, including my acting as his production assistant in RTÉ, our teamwork in *Riverdance* and our co-directorship of Tyrone Productions. In many ways, it is remarkable that our relationship was sustained because such a close working relationship can be quite tricky. It is not an easy thing to do over a long period of time. I think I speak for John as well, when I say that we would not both front such a major project as *Riverdance* again for the sake of our personal lives. A healthy compromise would be for one of us to front a project, with the other in support, on an alternating basis. We are currently working on a major classical music project and are also involved in two Broadway shows.

I see myself as both a businesswoman and a producer.

Business and creativity go hand in hand. Neither identifying a worthwhile business opportunity nor devising a wonderfully creative idea is alone sufficient to generate value. Creative people can invite the business support required to exploit their ideas, but they lose control and direction. Business people can solicit the creative talents of an artist but cannot extract the true value of artistic talent unless they understand the creativity.

Ireland and Irish people are brimming with creativity. Draíocht, a small cultural centre in Blanchardstown in which I am involved, is an example at the fringe of the Irish arts scene, while the Abbey Theatre in Dublin is a central example of excellence in Irish arts. However, I do not believe we have paid sufficient attention to the development of theatres and cultural centres in Ireland. Much greater progression of the arts is needed. As a major European capital, Dublin should have a proper opera house. The financial resources that our economic prosperity gives us now will not be around forever. It would be a great sadness not to devote money to building a national cultural centre that reflects credit on our deep history of literature and music and creates a legacy of this prosperous time in Ireland. For this, we live in hope.

CHRIS HORN

Founder and chairman, IONA Technologies

O ne week before I met with Chris Horn, chairman and founding CEO of IONA Technologies, I paid a research visit to the elegant IONA headquarters on the Shelbourne Road in Dublin. An engineering college friend met me in the cool and spacious atrium and took me to the heaquarters' rooftop restaurant. At Iona, the atmosphere is decidedly relaxed. There is no formal dress code, and people drift between tables, dispersing words of chat. The décor is calm and lush. The comfortable work environment is part of an effort to retain some of the world's best software developers and encourage their creative ability.

Creative ability has defined the company from the beginning. Foremost of the founding partners was Chris Horn. In 1991, he abandoned a career in academia to pursue commercialization of the technology he had been researching. This decision meant giving up the stability of university life, the steady flow of industrial grants and the comfort of knowing and controlling the forces brought to bear on his projects, namely the collective intellectual ability of his research teams. Six years after going into business, he floated IONA Technologies in the world's fifth largest IPO ever for a software company. The shares traded at the IPO valued the company at $240 million. In the three years after flotation the value quadrupled. Despite the downturn in the high-tech sector in 2000, his confidence in the future of IONA remains unshaken.

Chris Horn promotes an egalitarian company culture, making time for each individual in the company and often chatting at length with employees about their work. When I met him at both his Shelbourne Road offices and subsequently at IONA's US headquarters, just west of Boston, Massachusetts, I was struck by his soft-spoken and relaxed manner. He chose his words delicately, weighing each phrase carefully as he explained why he had left a comfortable career to invest so much in the risk of starting and sustaining IONA.

Belief and opportunity

At the early, start-up stage of IONA Technologies, I firmly believed that the venture could succeed. I had a strong belief in our ability and our knowledge. Our aspirations that these distinct advantages would make it work were high. My partners, Annraí O'Toole and Seán Baker, and I knew that we had a once in a lifetime opportunity and that we had to seize it.

The opportunity for our venture lay in the emergence of new technology standards in an area known as 'object-based computing'. Our belief in the venture was based on our assessment of how the industry at large was positioned to take advantage of these new standards. We studied the major players in the industry and saw that they were hesitant and hanging back from acting on the new technology. A strong and unfulfilled customer demand for this object technology existed. Most importantly, we shared a comprehensive knowledge of this technology, particularly in relation to building prototypes. In a worst-case scenario of unsuccessful product development, we could resort to consulting and training in this field or even return to the university environment and still make a good living. Since even the downside was comfortable, we felt we had everything to gain and little to lose by developing new products with IONA.

The timing was perfect. The more we got into it, the more we realized how far the other players were behind and how much better our approach to object technology was. We all felt that we had done our time in Trinity College Dublin and wanted to move on. The choice was to enter the industry either as consultants and trainers or by forming a venture. We took the most exciting route.

We were excited and enthusiastic about our chances of succeeding with the venture, but I was constantly reminded of the period when I undertook my doctoral studies in 1983. At that time, I was terrified that I would open a scientific journal and read that a researcher somewhere else had just completed and published the research I was working on. In the same way, I would come to work at IONA early each day with an expectant dread of seeing a press announcement that some other start-up had released a product that duplicated what we were trying to develop. However, that terror fuelled our determination and actually provided a good incentive to work very fast. There was always a sense that 'Tempus fugit' – 'Time flies.'

If there was one crucial success factor in achieving a successful start-up of IONA, it was having a trusting initial team that worked together coherently. We approached every aspect of our work on a collective basis rather than with disjointed individualism. We shared our thoughts, inspirations and concerns. Working without this coherency would have denied us the ability to talk to each other openly, honestly and supportively. The fact that the initial team had complementary skills increased our chances of achieving what we wanted. Seán

Baker was, at the time, a classical academic – highly analytical and theoretical, and a very good technologist. Annraí O'Toole, on the other hand, was fundamentally entrepreneurial, business-orientated and finance-driven. He could stand before an audience and captivate them with his enthusiasm for the technology. I myself was somewhere between Seán and Annraí. I am more academic than Annraí and more extrovert than Seán, so I was in a good position to balance and complete a very good team.

Out of academia

Like any young lecturers, we were so inexperienced in the ways of industry that we did not feel inhibited. Had we come with a deeper industry perspective, we might have been more reticent and cautious. As academics, we had a 'why not' attitude to everything we approached and just went for it. We did have some exposure to industry through our sponsored research and understood the operations and pressures of industry-sponsored research and development.

As academics, there were several things we needed to learn fast when we launched ourselves into the business world. Learning to deal with customers and financiers was the greatest personal challenge we faced at the outset. Initially, we ran IONA as a low-cost operation. We did not borrow money but bootstrapped it from our cash flow. When we began approaching venture capital firms in the United States, we came up against credibility issues, and dealing with the venture capital managers, face to face, in that context was hard. They asked tough and thorough questions, such as how we expected to be an Irish-based software company when our customers would be in the United States. In fact, personal challenges aside, the task of shifting our focus from a conservative European market to the open US market and raising the capital required to break into the US market proved to be the greatest challenge that IONA, as a company, faced.

Venture capital in Ireland

The availability of venture capital in Ireland has changed enormously in the last ten years. In 1991, when we first went searching for venture capital, the availability was minimal. A few Irish technology investments had collapsed in 1989 and 1990. The resultant sour taste compelled the Irish investment community to look to the United Kingdom and the Continent to make their investments. When we realized that they were not interested in investing in IONA, we looked to the States. We attracted very positive interest in Boston, but the venture capital people there could not fathom investing in Ireland. They thought it would be impossible to build a successful software company in Dublin, 3000 miles from the primary market.

Ten years later, Ireland commands the avid interest of venture capital firms from the United States, the United Kingdom and mainland Europe, all seeking to invest in new opportunities. We are an epicentre of information and communications technology innovation and enterprise. This emerging venture capital support brings its own dangers, however. In the United States, as much as 40% of research and development is currently funded by venture capital. Although I am glad that private capital investment is being directed toward many more creative activities, such as production of high-value-added goods, rather than being aimed solely at manufacturing facilities in Ireland, we should not become complacent and dependent on private capital funding of research and development, because it may become suddenly scarce in a time of recession. Research and development should be a fundamental tenet of government investment for future industrial development.

Good research and development is a hugely important differentiator in a competitive technology environment. The Irish company that invests in research and development is investing in its future and increasing not just its growth potential but its chances of survival. Often, government support for research and development in Irish companies creates something of an overly competitive spirit rather than a healthy, collaborative one. Universities, too, tend to compete fiercely for a limited source of funds, and in many instances, the funds are distributed inefficiently as a result. I think a closer link between government and universities would be constructive. Ultimately, a steady-state situation can be achieved whereby universities use the financial returns from commercialization of novel technologies to self-fund their research and development.

Encouragement of university enterprise

Commercialization of research and development is important to ensure a beneficial return from investment. Trinity College Dublin started the campus company scheme in 1984 to help bring research applications to the market. The university was keen to exploit results. At one time, some academics would approach the university seeking support and equity to launch a business. When they did not get it, they left and launched a business anyway. TCD realized it was losing both valuable expertise and the opportunity to become involved in successful businesses. Now a promoting officer vets each business proposal and gives seminars to explain the scheme and the opportunities of bringing research to full fruition through commercialization.

Initially, the majority of worthwhile business opportunities came from work on drugs and pharmaceuticals in the biochemistry department. Several companies were set up and spun off. Soon other departments saw the virtues of the scheme. One interesting venture, called Maptec, manipulated satellite images and provided geographical mapping services. Launching campus companies is a great way to motivate and incentivize researchers, while also providing revenue for continued research.

Other Irish universities are implementing similar commercialization schemes, all of which have been inspired by similar activities in Stanford and the Massachusetts Institute of Technology (MIT). MIT has a tremendous facility for innovation. Its campus in Boston is a Mecca for top engineering and scientific talent, and the collective brainpower has resulted in breakthrough technological advances. In particular, I am impressed with the Boston-based MIT Media Lab, which recently opened a European research laboratory in Dublin. MediaLabEurope is the laboratory for the digital future. The combined student body and faculty will number 250 and form a highly creative environment. Research projects will address such things as the interconnection between bits, people and objects in an online world and the prospect of giving objects the intelligence to 'think'. For instance, by sensing the movements of their owners, devices such as fridges, toasters and doorknobs will be able to communicate with each other and solve local problems. It is exciting to think about. The theory is that setting up this facility in Ireland will encourage large multinationals to fund MediaLabEurope, which will in turn encourage additional domestic research. Furthermore, the technology advances made by MediaLabEurope will provide opportunities for new Irish technology enterprises to start up in order to exploit the technology breakthroughs that are achieved. The investment price is a steep one – the government is committed to investing some £130 million over ten years. Time will tell if it is a wise investment or one that might have been channelled directly, and more profitably, into purely Irish research initiatives in universities and domestic companies.

IONA benefitted from the TCD campus company scheme, and in March 1991 we received enough funding to start the company in a small 15- by 8-foot office on the campus. In these early Trinity days, we undertook various projects unrelated to the mission at hand. For example, we delivered courses on Fortran to the Irish Meteorological Office, ran C++ courses for ICL and the UK Customs Authority and worked on consulting projects for the EU.

IONA people

In the early years, we hired a lot of graduates straight from university. I found that this was to the detriment of maturity. As our organization has grown and acquired bigger customers, the demands on the quality of our worldwide operations and business process have become very high. Now we tend to hire people who have ten or fifteen years of experience and who bring greater maturity and expertise. Our Irish and US staff share a similar outlook. The same forces in the industry drive them. They are very creative in providing new technology solutions. There is a lot of movement and interaction between Dublin and Boston, so we are well integrated and speak the same language.

Quite a few people join us with a view to understanding how a company such as ours works, with the intention of doing something similar one day themselves. IONA has provided a launching-pad for at least fifteen new companies. That reflects a tremendous enthusiasm and sense of enterprise in the people who work for us. I am delighted to see these new companies launch themselves independently into the fray of Ireland's rich new enterprise culture. It is good to know that we hired young people with the spirit and desire to create something new, turning innovative ideas into commercial successes and showing the grit and determination to set out in enterprises of their own. IONA benefitted from that same spirit while they worked here, and I wish them every bit of luck on their own. Many of those who have started their own companies felt that a company of 800 people was too big. They preferred to work with 5, 10 or 15 people. Now that IONA is established, we cannot afford to take the type of risks we took in the early days. We have built safety nets and find that some people are not prepared to stay in a safe environment where we will not place an 'all or nothing' bet on their ideas.

One company for which I have great hopes for the future is Cape Clear. The three founders, Chief Executive Officer David Clarke, Chief Operating Officer John McGuire and Chief Technical Officer Hugh Grant, are all former executives of IONA. Annraí O'Toole, co-founder of IONA, and Colin Newman, former vice-president of marketing at IONA, also left the company in late 2000 to join Cape Clear as executives, with Annraí taking a leading role as executive chairman. Cape Clear are entering a new area of Internet development by providing infrastructure technology that will enable Internet applications to interact more freely, creating in essence an 'invisible Internet'. In April 2000, Cape Clear generated first-round funding from institutional investors of $2 million, and IONA subsequently made a minority investment. Cape Clear is just one example of countless new Irish high-tech enterprises that are exciting to watch.

Other people join us because it is an opportunity to work with a leader in the software technology industry. They have the chance to develop interesting software in what is still a relatively small company by global standards. All the people who join us will have one thing in common – strong customer focus. They will work on products that will see the light of day in a large market. We are not yet rich enough and do not have enough surplus resources to be able to just play with something that will not be presented to the customers.

Terror, excitement and evolution

I could not replace the experience of setting up IONA and competing in the marketplace. We have been subjected to extremes of elation and deflation. The year 1993 was critical for us. We made our first product launch at the Object World trade show in the Moscone Center, San Francisco. We had purchased a booth in Dublin and shipped it to San Francisco, and it promptly fell down when assembled on the day before the show opened. We effectively bet our balance sheet on the launch of the product. We had very few cash reserves at the time, and if the product had been unsuccessful, we would have had to fold. We felt a mixture of terror and excitement, but the product launch went very well, to our relief.

By December 1993, we had grown to about 11 staff and had attracted strong interest from the Motorola Iridium project, which was building a global constellation of low-earth-orbit satellites for telecommunications. Sun Microsystems also started talking to us and were interested enough in our capability to invest $600,000 for a 25% stake in the company. Forbairt (now Enterprise Ireland) simultaneously stepped up with matching funding, based on the first 56 jobs we would create. We then severed our links with TCD as a campus company and moved to more spacious 4,000-square-foot offices in the same building as Sun Microsystems in Dublin. IONA started to expand rapidly and opened an office in San Francisco in spring 1994, relocating to Massachusetts the following autumn. By the spring of 1996, the company had grown to about 180 staff and had profitable revenues in the region of $8 million for the previous year. We won some big customers such as Boeing and Hong Kong Telecom.

The question was, What next? We had intensive discussions with Sun Microsystems about our future, and at one stage they offered to buy us outright. We rejected the offer both financially and strategically. Ultimately, Sun agreed to take the company public, and in February 1997 we had a tremendously successful stock market flotation. Sun sold out their entire stake and raised $60 million in the process – a phenomenal 100 times their original investment. Since then, our rapid growth rate has not slowed down, and I believe that our public status has given us additional credibility as a player in our market.

The excitement has continued as the company has grown. Winning large contracts, out-performing our competitors, and making our initial public offering have generated the same kind of buzz. But has it always been enjoyable? No. There have been some desperate and dreadful moments and a lot of tension and fear. We have faced very angry customers and extremely tough competitive forces. We missed a quarter in 1999 with below-target results, to the great disappointment of our staff and our investors.

There is a strong element of emotion in business. I was more passionate in the early days, but I was also more deflated by disappointments. I have had to learn to be more philosophical on a daily basis and get neither too excited nor too deflated to remain on an even keel. The ups and downs are too stressful.

The key success factors in sustaining the growth of our business have been both external and internal. External factors include ensuring that we innovate continually in order to generate products and associated services that consistently surpass our customers' expectations. Internally, the key success factors have been our commitment to maintaining a high morale among the employees of the company, our efforts to ensure that we have the right managers in the right positions at the right times, and our determination to manage our increasing turnover intelligently by dedicating sufficient funds to research and development in order to fuel future growth.

I have now taken more of a background role in the day-to-day operations. As chief executive officer, I was very much involved, almost micromanaging operations. Then we appointed Barry Morris as chief operation officer. The essential contract between us was simple. We would draw up an annual budget with projected revenue and profits, and he would make it happen. That left me free to concentrate on strategy. Barry was subsequently appointed chief executive officer. Since going public, we have delegated more and more. Now the founders manage seven people, while our executives effectively run the company for us.

The evolution toward this role allows me to undertake more activities outside IONA. My priority is my family. I can reduce the stress between company life and family life and spend more time with my wife and four children. I have two boys and two girls, the eldest of whom is fourteen. I have already spent too many years away travelling. However, there is little I would have done differently, given the chance again. Perhaps I would have handled some people issues differently, in circumstances in which we have let people go. By and large, though, if I had not started IONA, there would without doubt have been another venture.

Success and skills

IONA is, of course, only one of an ever-increasing number of Irish company success stories that reflect a phenomenal progress in Irish enterprise in the last fifteen years. It is a huge challenge to build indigenous multinationals, with national and international headquarters, that are leaders in their industries. Yet Ireland has produced numerous examples of successful indigenous enterprises, including Trintech, the Kerry Group and Ryanair, which have flourished and excelled in recent years and continue to grow in strength and reputation. Who would have believed this possible less than two decades ago when Ireland strained under the weight of exorbitant national debt, a depressed economy and unemployment that drove hundreds of thousands of young people from our shores. Today, Ireland has undergone a remarkable transformation to achieve almost full employment and a growing national surplus, thus becoming a shining economic beacon by which both developing and developed countries around the world guide their own economies.

The question arises: How will Ireland's transformation story unfold over the next two decades? We have every reason to be confident without being complacent. A consensus is gathering momentum that improving efficiency lies at the heart of sustaining a national competitive advantage. An efficient nation has attractively priced labour, raw materials, transportation, capital equipment and energy supplies; a reasonable rate of taxation; and a high level of productivity – productivity being the amount of goods produced for a given amount of raw materials. Producing goods and services that are consistently higher in value than those produced elsewhere also generates competitiveness. In Ireland, we have managed to maintain efficiency in productivity and to maintain attractive taxation of corporate and manufacturing profits. However, transportation costs and the cost of labour have been increasing steadily.

A potentially shackling challenge that Ireland faces is the increasing need for skilled workers. I had the privilege of chairing the state-sponsored Expert Group on Future Skills Needs and gained valuable insights into the skills needs that Ireland faces today and will encounter in the future. IONA's ability to grow in Ireland depends critically on the availability of skills in sufficient quantity to meet the needs of its business. The same is true of every small and large company in Ireland. On a national level, matching the supply of skills with the potential future demand is a complex exercise, yet, in my mind, it will be the critical factor in ensuring continued rapid economic growth and in maintaining competitiveness. If we can accurately estimate skills needs and increase the supply of those skills, we will avoid labour-market and consequent wage-cost pressures. The reality is that there is currently a serious shortage of skilled workers, and labour capacity is essentially static. Furthermore, there is a large element of uncertainty about the quantity and type of skills required four years hence, and the time delay in supplying new skills is from one to four years.

There can be very little doubt that a focus on creating highly skilled and highly paid jobs is needed. The availability of a skilled pool of labour has undoubtedly been a major factor in the economic boom we are currently enjoying. However, this pool of labour has now been deployed, and future growth potential is constrained as a result of the resultant shortage of skills. The globalization of the information technology industry means that companies will locate wherever the skills are available. If Ireland cannot provide the required workers, companies will go elsewhere, and it will be a very simple, clinical and swift decision for them. Skills availability is an opportunity as well as a potential problem.

The skills availability issue in Ireland is complicated by demographic trends. The number of school-leavers is declining. The supply of school-leavers for further education will therefore need to be augmented by people from other sources, such as immigration, retraining and people returning to work.

The emergence of the information society affects every business, and the demand for technologists does not come from the IT sector alone. If Ireland is to fulfil its high growth potential, the average annual demand for engineering and science technologists alone will be 8,300, according the studies we undertook. Including new educational initiatives planned by the government, the projected annual supply of technologists is only 5,400. The annual shortfall of some 3,000 is a threat to Ireland's ability to continue growing with the success it has experienced in recent times.

There are several ways in which promotion of education might meet this shortfall. Promotion of conversion courses and part-time courses can increase the supply of professionals through a process of 'up-skilling'. The number of places in full-time university technology courses needs to be increased, and education courses for technicians can be accelerated. The completion rates of technology courses are 85% at degree level and 65% at technician level. Higher completion rates could increase the annual supply of technologists by over 500, increasing skill supply in a very cost-effective way.

It is easy to place the responsibility for the increase in skills on the government, but Irish enterprise has its role to play also. Companies should develop learning programmes for the staff and provide fees for further education, as well as introducing staff release programmes and providing input into lecturing. It is for their own future benefit that companies should contribute to tackling the skills shortage problem.

Thirst and belief

I do believe that we can overcome such constraints on growth and that Ireland will continue to grow as it has done. Government, employers and trade unions can work cohesively to ensure a constructive growth. I believe, however, that the future is really in the hands of Irish individuals. It is Irish people, indigenous and warmly adopted, who can and will ensure a successful economy through their enterprise. Enterprise resides in the Irish gene, although it has been dormant until recent times. A new confidence has encouraged people to emulate the growing number of Irish successes and, in turn, set a new example of world-class enterprise themselves. Indeed, I believe there is enterprise in my own genes. It is less a case of wanting to work for myself than of needing to quench a thirst to create something new.

I believe that Irish people have the ability to build international companies that will make Ireland as successful as Silicon Valley. That was something I set out to prove with IONA when the US venture capital people said it could not be done in Dublin. I told them to 'watch this space'. I believe in letting people try roles and tasks they have not tried before. I myself had little experience in building and running a company.

If people have the commitment and enthusiasm for something new, then I encourage them to have a go and produce their best.

Finally and most importantly, I believe in enjoying my pastimes. I met my wife while windsurfing at Blessington, Co. Wicklow. My free time is sacred to me. In fact, though I am not avid about any one pastime in particular, and often gladly spend weekends as a taxi-driver, bringing my children to parties and matches, I do love open spaces, walking and fishing. Remoteness is great for perspective – what a welcome contrast from world centres of busy commerce, such as New York's Wall Street district or, indeed, Dublin city.

EDDIE JORDAN

Founder and CEO, Jordan Grand Prix

In the space of less than ten years, Eddie Jordan has established his Jordan Grand Prix motor-racing team as one of the biggest players in Formula One. From modest beginnings, he carried Jordan through debt-laden early years to create a business worth in excess of $200 million. In a big-business sport dominated by multinational corporations, Jordan is the only entrepreneur to launch a Formula One team and maintain control as its individual majority shareholder. His remarkable business success is due to his inherent flair for enterprise and his ability to look beyond traditional limits. Brought up in Rathgar in Dublin, Jordan studied medicine for a while before starting a career in banking, but he soon traded restlessness in a conventional profession for the excitement of the motor-racing circuit. He describes himself as a deal-maker and a hustler. He has cornered the Formula One market in negotiating lucrative partnerships. In 1998, he secured almost $40 million investment from global equity company Warburg Pincus, thereby becoming the first Formula One team to gain support from a financial institution. The financial muscle that this deal provides will propel the Jordan team to new levels of technical excellence and brand marketing. In 2000, Eddie Jordan was awarded Ireland's Ernst & Young Entrepreneur of the Year award.

Despite his exceptional business achievements, it is for his charisma, charm and love of life that Eddie Jordan is best known and liked. He creates an atmosphere of fun, sending up his team members in interviews, throwing rock concerts for his fans and playing the drums at impromptu music gigs. He has developed his own brand name in typical rock-and-roll style, launching an energy drink, EJ10, a glossy magazine, J, and a range of leisure wear. His skills in communication and promotion were undoubtedly a national asset during his short-lived appointment as Ireland's Tourism Sporting Ambassador in 1999.

An air of excitement surrounds Eddie Jordan. His personal energy and optimism are magnetic. In a room in the Westbury Hotel, he pops a bottle of champagne, pours two glasses and begins to tell his story.

Jordan Racing

Please understand me, motor racing is a drug. It takes up all of your time, and within reason, all other issues become secondary. It is something that completely and absolutely dominates your life. I live with it. I travel with it. It is a lifestyle. I have been accused of not being a serious operator in the past, and that hurt me. The truth is that I am very serious about racing, competing and winning – my team and I believe in what we are doing. The question is: How far can we go? The answer: I believe we can go all the way.

I have already come a long way. I began my working career as a clerk with the Hibernian Bank, now Bank Of Ireland. It was not an inspiring place to work. I found myself running small enterprises on the side to maintain some interesting activities as much as to make money. When a customer came to the bank looking for a car loan, they often left with a car from the selection of second-hand models I kept parked in the bank's carpark. From a young age I had a talent for spotting a business opportunity. I spent many weekends in my youth selling wool carpets and smoked salmon in Dublin's Dandelion Market. In 1970, Bank of Ireland had a series of strikes, and I took the chance to spend a summer on the island of Jersey. There, I tried my hand at kart racing and was converted to it with a passion. I was smitten by the speed. There was no way out. It was a serious adrenaline rush.

When I returned to Dublin, I bought a little 1000cc kart and practised in it at every opportunity. Two years later, I won the Irish Karting Championship and decided I had a future in racing. My parents thought I was crazy to give up a safe job in the bank. They kept telling me that I had had my fun and it was time to return to a proper job. My mother would get upset every time I broke my leg or had a bad crash and needed nursing at home. I did not stop. Every waking moment was filled with a passion to pursue greatness. I increased the power of my chosen car to a single-seat FF1600 vehicle and won three Formula Atlantic races in 1977. One year later, I won the Irish Formula Atlantic Championship and signed a deal with Philip Morris and Marlboro to join Team Ireland, which was based in Silverstone, England. I loved the racing, but other things in life began to change my thinking on the risks I was taking with my life every time I stepped into a racecar. I was married with one child, and my wife, Marie, was expecting a second. I felt selfish racing and decided to change from being a driver to a team owner. I set up the Jordan Motor Racing Team in 1979 and operated the outfit from a small lock-up unit at Silverstone. The following year, I retired from single-seater racing in order to concentrate on the business. For the next ten years, we raced in the Formula 3 championship and contested the Formula 3000 championship in the second half of the decade.

Although I believed I had the entrepreneurial skills to run the Jordan business, the early 1980s were very difficult years for Jordan Racing and especially for my family. There were years when I could not provide the security of a steady income. Some years, we would be flushed with success, but some years we would be out of luck and out of pocket. It was very difficult to attract good people to the team, and I did not have anywhere near the amount of money needed to be competitive at Formula 3000 level. At times, our financial difficulties brought us to our knees.

My chief mechanic, Rob Bowden, was killed tragically when the team's transporter crashed over a cliff. I was very shaken by this, and my gut instinct was to get out of the business. I went through a hard time, in which I questioned my own ability to handle the difficult times and pull the business through. After a lot of reflection, I came to the strong decision that I could make a success of the business and the racing team. I decided to stick with it, and the support of many friends who encouraged me gave me a lot of strength. Although this period was a dark and difficult one, we did enjoy some of the team's greatest feats, including a great win at the combined British and European round of the Formula 3 championship at Silverstone. Our drivers, Brundle, Byrne and Martin, picked up the top spots and beat the legendary Ayrton Senna that day to boot. I slowly built the character of the team, and success came Jordan's way again in 1987, when Johnny Herbert won the British F3, and a year later, when Jean Alesi took the F3000 title for Jordan.

Formula One

By the end of the 1980s, the Jordan team had won every category it had entered. The race successes and the graduation up the chain in formula championships built up secret hopes I had harboured for many years. From the first day I started in Formula racing, I always hoped and believed in the back of my mind that eventually I would break into the exciting world of Formula One. That was the jewel in the crown of motor racing. Entering Formula One would be a massive undertaking. The financial resources and the business, marketing and deal-making skills needed to compete at this level are massive. I had a self-belief and a passion for the sport and the business that I could not resist. In 1991 I established Jordan Grand Prix for Formula One racing.

We had a fantastic debut year. The team finished in fifth place in the World Championship. That year, Jordan also launched the Formula One career of an unknown 21-year-old German driver, Michael Schumacher, who would go on to become the world's best driver by the end of the decade. After one season with Jordan, Michael was snapped up by the Benetton team. I was devastated when he left. The early groundwork I had laid for a team was destroyed. I was too busy trying to pay the bills to let it devour me, and I was more upset at losing the £150,000 per race that Mercedes paid us every time Schumacher took to the circuit. That was a lot of money, and its loss put an even greater financial burden on us. At the end of the first season, we were a staggering £4 million in debt. For a period, I felt convinced that the business was at an end. Other racing teams were going to the wall in the recession of the early 1990s. Fortunately, Bernie Ecclestone, the man I regard as the father of motor sport, stepped in and provided financial support that enabled us to continue long enough to raise other sponsorship money and survive. I have never forgotten the belief he had in me.

Coming of age in sport and business

I slowly built the team and the business throughout the 1990s. It was a time when the sport was dominated by the giant teams of Williams, McLaren, Benetton and Ferrari. A good team needs a minimum of £65 million per year to enter the car constructors' championship, and less than £20 million of that will come from prize money and television coverage revenues. The Jordan team is the very last team in Formula One to have been built by an individual as opposed to a corporate partnership, and I have had to build the team from virtually nothing. Today, it is worth in excess of $200 million, and we are in serious contention with the Formula One heavyweights at last.

The late 1990s saw the coming of age of the Jordan team. Every year is a crucial year in Formula One, but 1998 was a watershed. We had a disastrous start to the year. At the end of May, we had won zero points and were on course to record our worst ever performance. My two top drivers, Damon Hill and Ralf Schumacher, brother of Michael, were becoming increasingly upset with the poorly performing Mugen–Honda engine in the Jordan cars. After May's Grand Prix in Monaco, Hill's frustrations boiled over in the paddock after a terrible drive that placed him eighth in the race. Trouble was brewing with Ralf Schumacher as other race teams began to try to lure him away from Jordan. The mounting losses and problems resulted in extremely low morale among the 150 people who worked for me, and this was made even worse by press rumours that I was thinking of selling the company. Nothing could have been further from the truth. I had invested my life and soul in Jordan, and I was desperately trying to find a way to lead the team out of a bad period. It was difficult to remain upbeat, but if I was to be a good leader, I knew I had to instil motivation and encourage my designers, engineers and drivers to reach a higher level of performance. As a leader, it was my job to make my team members believe in themselves.

I called a series of crisis meetings with my management team to see which changes we could make to improve our dismal record to date. I put a lot of energy into encouraging my drivers to believe in their ability, and I tried especially hard to divert the media heat that they were feeling. By midsummer, we started to pick up points, but the sweetest moment came in late August. Damon Hill and Ralf Schumacher sped home in first and second place in the Belgian Grand Prix. It was a nail-biting finish and a result that realized a life-long ambition. At last, Jordan had won a Grand Prix race.

I have always tried to look beyond the conventional limits in my business. For years, I had been developing skills in securing sponsorship and marketing the team. Success in these areas had brought us the funds and credibility needed to become Grand Prix champions. There was one more level to reach. I wanted Jordan to challenge the heavyweight Formula One teams for the overall championship and constructors' title. In order to do this, I needed a serious injection of funds. I considered floating the company on the stock exchange and also entered partnership discussions with Honda. Both ideas fell through because of unsatisfactory price negotiations. I looked beyond the usual collection of car, oil and brand retail companies for investment. At the end of 1998, I signed a deal with the US investment group Warburg Pincus and sold a minority share of Jordan. The investment was a groundbreaking one, as Jordan became the first team to gain investment from a financial institution. I remained the chief executive and majority shareholder and had a new currency to expand the business and plan future successes. A Warburg Pincus executive joined the Jordan board and added a great deal of expertise, but I made it clear from the start that I would stay in control. The funds allowed us to invest in high-tech facilities for designing and building more competitive cars, which ensured that we could continue to attract and incentivize top drivers. The deal also brought a new security to my family, which had endured so much financial uncertainty for years.

Although 1998 had been a great year, 1999 would prove to be our most successful ever. Ralf Schumacher had duly left us, and I had signed another promising German, Heinz-Harald Frentzen, to partner with Damon Hill. In June, Frentzen won the Grand Prix for Jordan at Magny-Cours in France. A year earlier, the Belgians had played the wrong national anthem after our victory, so it was sweet at last to hear 'Amhrán na bhFiann' played into a wet and windy French sky. Frentzen won spectacularly again in Monza, Italy, in September and boosted the Jordan team up the points table. These wins gave Jordan its best ever championship year: the team took third place in the constructors' championship, with Frentzen in third place in the drivers' championship. For the first time in a decade, a new team had broken the McLaren–Williams–Benetton–Ferrari monopoly at the top of Formula One.

Deal-maker and manager

I have developed and learnt so much over the years in Formula One. I am not a very detailed person. I am not even a very organized person. In fact, I do everything on the hoof. This means that I have had to develop good communication skills and an ability to negotiate and form alliances spontaneously. I have also learnt to delegate tasks that can be better carried out by others and that leaves me the freedom to tackle important issues with efficiency. These days, in fact, I delegate virtually everything, with the exception of meeting new prospective partners and tying down commercial contracts. I would consider myself to be in the fine bracket of 'salesman'. There is a big difference between a marketer and a salesman, although the two are very often associated with each other. I believe that a brilliant marketer is not often a brilliant salesman. A deal is not over until the ink is dry. Marketers might be fantastic promoters of new ideas. They might create great packages and present deals with direct and polished eloquence. They might capture the attention and even agreement of partners or customers. However, a marketer often forgets that there comes a moment when it must be clear that the deal is concluded and irreversible. A great marketer can often fall short of that crucial point. A great salesman always closes the deal. In the many years of negotiating with sponsors, agents and stakeholders, I have always tried to keep this in mind.

It is very important to enter a deal negotiation with an sense of fairness and flexibility from the start. The one type of person that I just cannot do business with is an inflexible person with a closed mind. Every successful negotiation starts with a good under-standing of the requirements of the other party. I try to put myself in their position and feel what their upper and lower limits are and what the break point is at which they will walk out. I also have a clear understanding of what my own limits are. How much or little will I settle for? What is my starting position? What concessions am I prepared to make, and if I make a concession, what will I seek in exchange? What final giveaways do I have that can clinch a deal with the other party? Negotiation can involve a lot of hardball tactics, but there has to be enough flexibility on both sides for a settlement to be reached. If both parties are willing to do a deal, then they will find a way to make it happen. I cannot cope with deal-makers who just dig their heels in and stop at that. I have seen too many negotiations where people waste breath and energy trying to conclude a deal in vain because the two sides are diametrically opposed and unwilling to meet on common ground.

Psychology, body language and environment play a huge part in determining the outcome of a negotiation. Understanding the mood of the other negotiating party in the first minutes of a dialogue can be crucial in knowing how to play to their thought process. The nature of body gestures and even voice intonation can raise or lower the level of comfort and trust between negotiating parties. Very importantly, the setting and timing of a negotiation can play a role in the way a deal is struck. Where people are sitting in relation to each other, what food you have prepared to eat, whether it is morning, afternoon or evening time all help to determine the type of environment – positive, friendly, tense or tough – that you want to create.

I consider Bernie Ecclestone to be a great negotiator and a great businessman for whom I have huge admiration. He is tough yet approachable. He is an excellent people person, and I find many occasions to talk to him about my business. He has achieved all he has from nothing. One important thing that I learnt from him is the ability to say no. So many people find it very hard to say no and end up in a situation that they do not like and that is spiralling out of their control. Perhaps it also becomes easier with age, but I find that I can say no to things with far less effort now, and this saves me a lot of trouble.

I do not like to be trapped behind a desk. I am at my best when I am out and about and networking. That is the nature of my managerial style. I have learnt not to get hung up on expectations, and in that way I do not get affected when things do not work out. With age, I have become more philosophical and just let things happen, rather than forcing things in a particular direction all the time. Another factor that helped me to gain a philosophical comfort was my good education and early work experience. Working in a bank gave me very good working discipline. I was in a position where there were a lot of rules that could not be broken, and if they were, trouble would result. Although many rules may seem quite mundane or even stupid at times, they serve the purpose of creating and maintaining discipline and control. Good rules are a necessary part of the function and structure of any business or sport. When I was in very deep financial troubles in my early Formula One years, I reverted to my understanding of the banking system and how it worked. Knowing the rudiments of banking and not being afraid of the financial accounting I had to do was an advantage I was fortunate to have.

One of the key elements of the business for me is staff. I get very upset when somebody leaves, and I question if I treated them well or if I should have paid them more money. There is a lot of movement in our business. If there is one thing I have learnt from the Schumacher brothers, it is that a contract can be broken if the will is there. Employers are in a difficult position. They have to live a contract to the letter and oblige and humour staff in every way. If an employer does anything wrong and annoys an employee who is hot property, the employee has every chance to get out of his contract, irrespective of its length. The best drivers are in huge demand. Jordan pays out about £5 million each year to its drivers.

Most of the senior people who are with me today have been part of the team for more than ten years, and that is quite unusual in our business. There are lots of people in the team who have been with me through ups and downs. I would be devastated if any of them left, because I feel that we are part of a family. I want to be sure that I create a business that takes care of my staff. They do a tremendous job, and I want them to be rewarded for the value that they bring to the team.

Tourism Sporting Ambassador

I was elated to be appointed Ireland's Tourism Sporting Ambassador in 1999 by the Minister for Tourism, Sport and Recreation, Dr McDaid. It was a great honour. When I heard the news, I knew it would be a role that I would really enjoy and could dedicate a big effort to. Apart from obvious activities such as advertising Irish sporting events at race meetings and wearing Bord Fáilte logos, I anticipated travelling to different countries to promote Irish sporting teams and Irish venues, increasing awareness of such major events in Ireland as the Ryder Cup and leveraging my knowledge of sponsorship and financial investment in sporting activities.

There was also much room for promotion of the sport I know most about. With investment, the karting circuits at Mondello Park or the Phoenix Park could be transformed into top Formula 3 circuits or even top Formula 3000 circuits. Ireland could be promoted as a centre of training for new international drivers. It would also be a way to produce sensational new Irish drivers. Holland's biggest festival is the Formula 3 festival, held each year in Zandberg. Every August, hundreds of thousands of people converge on the city, and the tourism generates a large source of income for the Dutch government.

I saw the position of Ireland's Tourism Sporting Ambassador as an extension of a role I had already played in the previous decade, and, to some extent, I felt the award was a recognition of the many activities I had undertaken to promote Ireland and its sporting culture and achievements. We have always tried to promote Ireland in racing and are proud that the Jordan team is known throughout the world as an Irish team. With all our staff based in Silverstone in Britain, it would have been very easy to have adopted a British image, but that was never my intention or my style. I have been very insistent on the Irish element.

I was extremely upset when the title was taken away. I believe it was taken away at a time when I was performing well beyond the call of duty at all of the activities I had been asked to do. I was just warming to the role and had established many contacts through my visits to foreign countries and embassies. Ultimately, anti-smoking lobbies and sentiment, which argued that the Jordan racing team's sponsorship by tobacco companies undermined national anti-smoking campaigns, made it very difficult for Minister McDaid to extend my term after one year. I could understand the pressure that the minister faced, but I could not see the merit in the argument of the anti-smoking people. I was appointed Tourism Sporting Ambassador, not the Jordan racing team ambassador, and there is a clear distinction between me as an individual and the racing team that I own and manage. I understand the sensitivity about the tobacco industry, but I think the lobbyists who instigated the controversy over my position did not make any effort to try to understand the opportunities being created by the ambassadorship. I am enormously proud to be Irish and wanted to use the position to create great benefit for Irish sport. I feel a responsibility not only to Irish people in Ireland but also to the thousands in other countries around the world who will eventually come back home greater and better people and with whom I have a strong connection.

Entrepreneur of the Year

Early in September 2000, I was chatting to Denis O'Brien in Dublin, and he said to me very casually, 'Why don't you come to dinner while you're in town?' I did not know whether he had something special in mind or not. I thought we were going to go to a Bob Dylan rock concert because Dylan was in town that night, and I remember saying how much I would love to see him live. I learnt afterwards that it turned out to be a very special Dylan concert, because he played to an intimate 400 people in the Vicar Street venue. In the event, Denis O'Brien took me to the Berkeley Court Hotel, where the Minister for Finance, Charlie McCreevy, was hosting the Ernst & Young Entrepreneur of the Year awards. I had every intention of slipping out to catch the last half of Bob Dylan live until my name was called out as the overall winner of the award!

In all seriousness, I was overjoyed to win the award. It was great because it was so different for me to win a business award. I had won small awards for driving or sporting awards with the Jordan team, but to win an entrepreneurship award in Ireland, a country that is so far ahead in enterprise, was thrilling. I was honestly surprised to win it, because there were so many great young companies emerging with amazing enterprise leaders driving their success, companies such as Parthus and Riverdeep. I would have imagined that these people were far better entrepreneurs in the truest sense of the word because motor racing has such a different perspective. Perhaps I had an advantage because motor racing is a very visual and high-profile sport. It is very obvious whether or not a racing-team leader has made the best use of the resources at hand and whether the team has achieved success. When the master of ceremonies announced that I was the overall winner, I was quite pleased that the citation made reference to the fact that I was an entrepreneur who had seen the dark side of enterprise. I did indeed come from the dark side. I had struggled without money for several seasons, and I think the award recognized my survival of difficult times as much as it recognized the achievement of recent successes. There are a lot of very bright young guys in Ireland who are making fortunes for themselves but who have never known the dark side.

Being Irish is a big help in business. Irish people have a very strong human side. They have an ability to talk in any type of circumstance and to any nature of person. If the discussion is contentious, they can be contentious; if it is serious, they can be serious; if it is compassionate, they can be compassionate. Irish people can wear very many different hats and seem to be able to adapt to whatever situation they face in a natural and comfortable way. This ability to communicate is a wonderful gift.

Being Irish has definitely helped me. I feel I have been accepted with warmth in Britain. I think that this is because Irish people are considered to be good fun but also hard-working. The Celtic Tiger success in Ireland has created a new reason for the popularity of the Irish. Irishness is equated with street credibility now, as distinct from the aged association with bricklaying 'micks'.

F1 sport and business

Motor racing is as much a business as it is a sport. The number of fans creates a huge market. More than 400 million people watch each race live – a staggering figure. Major industrialists and multinational companies want more and more involvement in motor sport. If they are not already a part of the action, they want to be. All the car manufacturers want to be included. A huge array of telecommunications companies are getting involved. Old-economy businesses, new-economy businesses, small, medium-sized and large businesses are all clamouring to get in. Major names have been staked on the sport and a wide range of industries are now represented, including the electronics world of Compaq and Sony, the oil world of Shell and Mobil, and the tobacco companies. There is huge money in it. The rewards for teams and drivers are enormous. It is a travelling extravaganza that grows stronger and stronger each year.

Television and enhanced technology has definitely brought motor sport further into the business realm because of the huge viewing figures. Television has brought the sport so intimately into homes across the world that it has become something of a soap opera. Motor-sport purists who have been involved in the sport for a long time sometimes get irritated because the business pressures have changed the essence of the sport. Things have definitely changed, and I am happy to have changed with them. I feel as if I have been part of a revolution. Formula One is far more commercially focussed, but its popularity has soared, and that can only be a good thing for the championship. Despite the commerciality, when the cars are on the circuit on a championship Saturday or Sunday, it is without doubt a sport. That is when the adrenaline flows, the nerves are on edge and every sense is heightened in excitement.

To this day, I do not sleep a lot the night before the first race of the season, because it is such a key race. It gives me a very clear idea of how the team is going to perform throughout the season. The qualifying race on the Friday night is particularly unnerving because I do not know where the car is going to qualify. After qualification, I can tackle the race strategy. Once the race itself has started, I set about the business of talking the drivers through the laps, but all through the race, the adrenaline is pumping. I believe in living life to the full. During a race, I am right on the brink, and my heart is hoping that the drivers live up to that belief and go all the way.

LOUISE KENNEDY

Fashion designer; Founder and owner,
Louise Kennedy fashion label

*T*he Louise Kennedy fashion label is one of Ireland's finest-
quality exports. Louise is a woman and she is a brand. She
is young, talented, stylish and successful, and she has exquisite
taste in fabrics. Louise recalls that from a very early age, she was
passionate about fabrics and their colours. As a student in the
Grafton Academy, she reverted from her chosen discipline of
interior design to her youthful passion and turned her hand to
fashion design. Only weeks after graduation, an unexpected
turn of events led her to launch her own fashion designer brand
on the back of a small bank loan. She won national recognition
with the Late Late Show/Ulster Bank Designer of the Year
award. Her career blossomed thereafter, and her annual London
Fashion Week and catwalk shows have won her an international
reputation. At her Georgian headquarters on Merrion Square in
Dublin and her boutique in London's Belgravia district, she has
dressed such well-known women as Meryl Streep, Mary
McAleese, Cheri Blair, Gwyneth Paltrow and Minnie Driver.

Razzmatazz start

I had a running start in the Irish fashion industry. I never
intended to launch my own label straight away. I knew I would
quite like to end up with my own label at some stage, but it

certainly was not a priority of mine to go straight into a start-up programme. I was given the opportunity to showcase my fashion design work at an arts college graduate show that also featured well-established, mainstream Irish designers. It was a big show, and the buyers from all of the country's clothes stores and boutiques attended. I agreed to do a capsule of twelve designs for the show. I had every intention of making my designs for this one show and then leaving Ireland to try to get some work experience in New York. However, my plans changed utterly when a Brown Thomas buyer approached me at the show and said she would like to see my full collection by private exhibition. At the time, I was too stunned to think of the logistical implications of such an exhibition. It was too great an opportunity to turn around and say, 'Actually, I have other plans.' So I decided to go with the flow and agreed.

I did not have a showroom in Dublin at the time, so I rented a room in the Westbury Hotel. I created a full catwalk show – the full razzmatazz. The Brown Thomas buyer was very impressed, and she wrote an order for the label there and then. It was very brave of her to invest her budget in an unknown label of an unknown graduate who was just emerging into the marketplace. The signing can be attributed more to luck than to any plan of mine, but it would have been crazy to turn down a break like that. Who knows what might have happened had I boarded a plane for New York? I might have taken a different tangent and might never have come back. I am happy with my choices. That signing took place in 1984, and today Brown Thomas is still one of the strongest supporters of the Louise Kennedy label.

I started the business from an overdraft position. I took out a loan of £10,000 from the bank and asked my father to act as guarantor for me. I figured that the £10,000 would be ample to facilitate my first collection for Brown Thomas. It was unusual for a designer with my lack of design experience and non-existent brand label to trade at such a prestigious store as Brown Thomas. However, with both parents well established in the clothing retail trade and with my own determination, I knew I could be a fast learner and justify the faith placed in me.

My parents' experience in the retail business was an enormous help to me. I learnt an awful lot from observing them at an early age, although I may not have been aware of it. From the age of ten or eleven, I was immersed in the daily happenings of the clothing industry. I knew how the infrastructure of the retail business was laid out and was impressed with the importance of forward planning and budgets. I also understood the nature of seasonal cycles. I gained an appreciation of the basics of marketing through asking such questions as: Who exactly are the customers? In what market segment are they? What are their needs? How can a product meet these needs, and through which channel should it be delivered? I also learnt the importance of delivering products that were to the same standard as samples and of delivering according to schedule, and I learnt the necessity of having back-up raw material. After my mother died, I spent half of my time in Dublin and the other half in Tipperary, working in the family business. My father had always worked on the finances of the business, so I learnt a lot from his expertise in that area. I attended overseas trade fairs and saw how the industry worked on an international level. My parents' example and teaching left me with a thorough knowledge of the inner workings of the retail trade. It was a solid grounding for starting my own business.

The Louise Kennedy label grew at a very slow pace after its initial launch. I rented my first office on South Anne Street in

Dublin's city centre. It was a time of recession in Ireland – the grim late 1980s – and a very different period from the brighter 1990s, when retailing was much stronger. I learnt so much from growing a business in hard times. Buyers are so cautious in a recession and never overspend, so market growth was static. As a result, I did not have to extend my range or take a chance on expanding to meet the demands of the marketplace. After each season, I re-invested all the profits in the business, and I was then able to hire assistants to work with me.

Our direct retailing channel was through a concession space in the Brown Thomas store on Grafton Street in Dublin. Having a concession allowed us to maintain control of our own selling area within the store and feed our inventory with a buffer of back-up stock. This is a large advantage compared with selling externally to a store. In an external deal, store buyers have a fixed seasonal budget and meet a designer twice a year to purchase clothes. In most cases, their budget will be replenished only once a season, so if the store sells out a particular designer brand, there is no way of replacing the clothes and increasing sales. With a concession space, a designer estimates the stock to be sold in a season but can replenish the stock every week or every day as necessary. Having my own Brown Thomas concession was a terrific start.

Designer of the Year

Winning the *Late Late Show*/Ulster Bank Designer of the Year award in 1989 came at a very important time for me. The Irish economy was starting to change for the better, making a positive impact on consumer spending in the fashion trade. I could never have raised the amount of money needed to secure the exposure that the award gave me. Television is surely the best medium to reach a wide audience, and the benefit that I derived from the *Late Late Show* broadcast was immense. People throughout Ireland, who had never before heard of the Louise Kennedy label, suddenly had a great degree of confidence in the brand and in the clothes. In the weeks following the show, I was inundated with new accounts. National newspapers and magazines also took an interest and wrote feature articles on my work. The impact of the award was clearly noticeable on the sales graph of the label.

I was also very fortunate with the timing of Mary Robinson's inauguration as President of Ireland. This was especially important for the label from an international standpoint, because there was so much interest in the election of Ireland's first female president. The international press representatives covering the event were asking, 'What will the president be wearing for the inauguration?' 'Who is Louise Kennedy?' Although this was not a major focus for Mary Robinson, her wearing one of my outfits generated a great deal of international interest in the label. I had also become a member of the British Designers Association and was invited to my first season at the prestigious London Fashion Week. The exhibition was housed in a stately two-tiered marquee at the Natural History Museum. Each designer had a stand just like the stands in a trade exhibition. Once again, a lot of the magazines placed my work in feature articles as a result of their interest in the collection at the Fashion Week. The confluence of all of these events marked a new high point for the business.

Little glamour

Despite these good publicity breaks, the very early stages of my business were hard. Monitoring credit given to international wholesale accounts and meeting our bank repayments was a challenge. The nature of the clothing industry also left me very dependent on a chain of other people, particularly the manufacturers with whom I had signed contracts. Working ahead, I always gave the factories deadlines and supplied the fabrics in an organized and timely way. However, I constantly needed to monitor the progress in the factories so that they would not let me down in meeting delivery deadlines. Downstream in the chain, buyers, who were under pressure to make a return per square foot on their floor, demanded that my collection always arrive exactly on the requested date. The constant pressure from all the interdependent relations and logistics hiccups that can happen along the way took a lot of the glamour out of the fashion business.

In 1993, my entire collection was stolen at the start of my second exhibition at the London Fashion Week. All the samples, 200 pieces in total, were stolen. The shipment was being delivered on New Bond Street, which is notorious for daylight robbery because of the amount of high-end, valuable paintings and clothing delivered on the street. The collection was in very large 10-foot hanging containers, and the clothes were simply taken out of the van and, instead of being sent in through the goods entrance, were shifted into another van and disappeared.

It was a huge shock. The oversight of security really frustrated me and added to the great upset of the loss of all the hard work. The level of work commitment that had gone into the collection was enormous. It was six months of my life. When a collection is shipped, you say, 'That's another season down', and you can hear the design team sigh with relief because the bedlam of the last two weeks of putting the collection together is over at last. The people involved in finance and pricing are also relieved to know that the collection is finally on the way to market and sure to generate returns. There are so many people depending on a collection, so it was devastating to have lost six months of work.

As a team we did not panic when we heard the news, because we knew it could be solved. This was crisis management in action. We sat down and talked about what could be saved. We agreed that we would have no Fashion Week that year, but we were determined to achieve one full month of selling. We negotiated an extension on our selling period, and everything fell into place. Everybody went to work fervently the following day. The response was quite incredible. Fortunately, 1993 was a year when the London catwalks were on fire. Designers were selling through their own offices and showrooms. This meant that static exhibitions, such as those at the London Fashion Week, had less impact on sales, and we could discount the damage of the loss. We managed to get 80% of the collection back together again and salvaged our existing clients, although we were not able to expand the business that particular season. The British press was very kind to us in the aftermath of the robbery, and we received huge coverage as a result of the theft. The heist of an entire designer collection at the start of Fashion Week became the biggest news story in London for a week. Although it was not the way I would have liked to develop the brand, the press recognition was very favourable. People wanted to know more about such a sought-after label.

Prima donnas

A good team can create a very calm environment in which any crisis can be met with the resolve necessary to deal with it. I have a great working relationship with my team, who are mostly female. We have our moments, but we are not afraid of hard work, and, on this occasion, everybody pulled together to sort out the problem. Loyalty is so important to me. It is something that has grown in the team over a long period of time. We do not have official titles here. People know their responsibilities and carry them out to the best of their ability. I need people who are prepared to get involved in every aspect of the business. The nature of the fashion business stretches work commitment well beyond the nine-to-five schedule and sometimes requires working extremely long days to meet deadlines. The people on my team each contribute to the vision of our creative design. I have twenty-three people working with me currently, which makes for a small but intimate environment in which communication is honest and very open. There is no room for prima donnas. I need people who will be able to plug into whatever tasks need to be done when they need to be done.

Building the label

In 1998, I decided that I needed to expand the business. We were working in downtown Dublin in the very heart of the clothing industry area, but we were very short of space. A large warehouse would have been practical and sensible, but a beautiful Georgian house on Merrion Square came on the market, and when I inspected it, I found that it suited our needs in every way. We opened our lifestyle salon in Merrion Square and established it as the flagship for the company. We also opened a boutique in the esteemed Belgravia fashion district in London, and we hope to open another two boutiques in the future.

The Louise Kennedy label has evolved with the size of the collection. In the beginning, I was very focussed on my first love of quality tailoring. I stayed very focussed on the quality of fabrics and ensured that the label never dropped its quality standard. While our early margins were small, our overheads were also small, so we were able to buy top-end fabrics and still remain competitive. I will always pay extra for that special metre of fabric or for a particular degree of quality. It is easy to cut corners and reap a higher margin, but in the long term, people's estimation of our label is directly proportional to the quality of our products.

The strongest competition came from established labels such as Armani and Donna Karan, which enjoyed high customer awareness and endorsement. These had enormous marketing teams and vast coverage in magazines and newspapers and on television. As an unknown label, we entered the market at a price level that was highly competitive. When customers experienced the fit and the quality, they were impressed and stayed with our collections. Clients who bought from our very first offering continue to support us every season. They have an expectation of the label that we strive to surpass year after year.

Our initial target market consisted of professional women. To understand the needs of this segment, we looked at such details as the work and recreation patterns of professional women. We translated their requirements and tastes into work clothes. As we grew in size and recognition, we moved from strict tailoring into the wider lifestyle market. We extended into evening wear, weekend wear and, finally, into all of the accessories that professional women need. For the last ten years, we have tried to reach further into the professional woman's wardrobe, trying to encapsulate her lifestyle and meet more of her demands. This approach has certainly helped us to focus on growth. Every season, more women are attracted to the collection, and our turnover has increased accordingly.

We have taken the brand outside of the fashion realm through our partnership with other high-end craftspeople and display our clothing designs alongside work from Tipperary Crystal and David Lindsey to encourage customers to visit our salon. There has been great synergy between the brands, which has generated increased interest and trade in the Louise Kennedy label. I was delighted when Tipperary Crystal approached me and asked if I would be interested in designing a select line of their crystal ware. It has been fantastic in terms of broadening my own brand and putting it into totally different markets. I panicked a little with the realization that drawing glass outlines was very alien to my experience of drawing for the human body and that a team of master cutters and designers were depending on my input. In the end, the task was not as unfamiliar as I had imagined, and I fell back on the tactile element of my visual sense. I imagine the proportions of a design as if I could touch them in my mind, and, in that way, I have a strong visual idea of what I want to create in physical form. Tipperary Crystal gave me carte blanche to create my design, specifying only that they wanted something contemporary for a very light cut. We worked very well together, and they let me push the boundaries on certain things, such as making a square cut, which they had initially argued was not technically possible. In my lack of technical knowledge of crystal-cutting, I kept asking, 'Why not?'

I made a design I felt very passionate about. The same principles apply to my fashion design as to my crystal design. I designed the crystal cup in relation to the stem in the same way that I would design the length of a jacket in relation to a skirt or a pair of trousers. The sight of a crystal-cut glass has to invoke the same feelgood factor as the touch and cut of a perfect garment. I got feedback from people who said that they saw the same handwriting in both my clothes and the crystal. In that way, I feel that I managed to widen the brand in a special context. There is no distinction between my brand and myself, because I invest so much of my own passion in my work. I could not put my name to something if I did not feel so strongly about it. I regularly receive requests to design for other craft labels and to create select products similar to the Tipperary Crystal line. I usually turn them down because I do not feel a strong sense of personal synergy with the products or brand.

Handwriting

There is no distinct Irishness in the handwriting of my clothes. In fact, in the very early stages in London, a lot of people thought we were an American company and thought the styling was quite American, and others presumed we were an Italian company because so much of the cloth is sourced in Italy. I do not weave any Celtic influences into my designs. The limit of traditional Irish influence in my design is my love of textured tweed, and yet I myself am wholly Irish.

Being an Irish designer at the start of the new century has an enormous advantage. Ireland's growth has captured the attention of the world, and Dublin is seen as such a cultural city. We have earned huge overseas interest on the fashion front, and Irish designers are featured regularly in international magazines. The international journalists who come to Ireland to capture the pulsating new Irish spirit describe a new avant-garde approach to fashion and style. Our brand has been added to that swell of excitement, and this has elevated our reputation and international exposure.

My handwriting is constant. I am not influenced by wild trends when I design a new season's collection. I have a knowledge of the people who will wear my clothes, and I tailor to their needs. I allow my handwriting to evolve as the market evolves. As tastes slowly change, I try to bring something new and fresh and exciting. The one thing that will differentiate my label from another and win a client's heart is that I always try to add a little twist to a classic cut. People look for something different in a label – something that will distinguish them from the mean. I love the challenge of making each new season's collection stronger, larger and better. I love devising new concepts for fabrics. The size and stature we have achieved allows us to work directly with the mills to develop completely new fabrics. That is very exciting because we are developing clothes from scratch – indulging in the magic of creating something from nothing.

I see myself as both a designer and a businesswoman. If I were one of a multitude of designers in a design company, I probably would not have had the exposure to the business and financial aspects of running the company. Running my own enterprise keeps me involved in both the designing and business sides every single day. Each part dovetails with the other and ensures the survival of my label. I must achieve excellence of design and creativity in my collection each season, but there is little point in turning out a terrific collection if I have overpriced it for the marketplace or if I have not controlled my production costs. I think I am at an advantage in straddling both the design and business disciplines because as the business and market needs change, I can adapt the nature of my collection in anticipation of these changes rather than reactively. In this way, I do not become lost in a polarized vision of a collection but can control it so that it becomes a vision shared by my clients.

I get a buzz out of increasing the profit margins of my

business. It is terrific to try new ideas in design and watch their effect in the margins generated. However, I prefer the freedom of the design side of my activities. I would rather face a blank sheet of paper and a pencil than deal with an accountant who wants to spend weeks going through the figures. My ultimate freedom results from having my own enterprise. I am in control of my design, my direction and my life.

Irish talent

I would advise any young designer setting out in the business to get some work experience abroad. The big fashion companies can offer an insight into the structure of the industry. There are so few companies in Ireland that offer a similar experience. Experience in a big Italian design company, for instance, will result in a solid understanding of the operations of the business in terms of the interdependence of the supply chain through the successive stages of materials provision, manufacturing and retailing. The big companies can also instil an ability to see the bigger picture and maintain a perspective in a profession in which it is often easy to become lost in the details. Maintaining an overview is crucial for designers so that they do not lose sight of the market for which they are designing. Big companies are also quick to recognize and reward talent, of which there is no shortage in Irish graduates.

With good industry experience, starting your own design company can be a thrilling experience. More and more Irish design graduates who left for the Continent are returning home to set up their own businesses. The economic climate in Ireland has never been better for encouraging new fashion businesses. Consumers are not afraid of buying, and their demand for high-end fashion is strong. New retail outlets being built in cities across the country provide new platforms for young designers to profile and market their work.

I am concerned about the production facilities for the fashion industry in Ireland. The shrinkage rate of Irish clothing manufacturing is in the region of 10% a year. Ten years from now, I will have no choice but to look abroad for manufacturing support, and this may ultimately lead to moving the brand out of Ireland. I see little investment in the industry to reverse this trend. Currently, the focus on investment in information technology, software development and biotechnology is so great that there is little breathing space for other industry segments. School-leavers are also strongly encouraged to partake in technology courses at third-level institutions in order to fill the skills shortage in these advanced-technology segments. As a result, interest in the clothing industry is waning, and fewer students are developing their artistic skills. The government and the industry federations need to take action now to revive the clothing industry. Lack of investment leaves very few Irish companies with the ability to handle the fabrics that are needed if we are to achieve the quality we want in our clothes. We have to be able to compete with producers of internationally renowned, high-quality goods.

Future fashion

I am very focussed on developing the Louise Kennedy label into a luxury-end brand. I predict that three or four very large companies will buy up the smaller companies and will dominate this end of the market. Small companies will find it difficult to survive on their own in the face of consolidated competition. A brand will need to have stand-alone shops in every major European and American city to compete successfully. To meet this challenge and enable the business to grow, we want to establish new retail outlets, expand the collection and focus strongly on gaining a reputation in the United States that will propel us to a bigger scale.

Significant investment in the company will allow us to grow in this way. A loan investment is too risky a platform for growth, so I am looking at the possibilities of a strategic partnership. A partnership that can provide complementary manufacturing and marketing capacity would be ideal. The possibility of partnership and growth is the greatest source of excitement for the brand, the company and myself. Who knows what the future holds?

For the present, nothing gives me more enjoyment than the feedback I get from my customers. I love to see a person try an outfit and to watch the pleasure they experience from wearing it. It is little moments like that that make it so worthwhile. I still feel the thrill that all designers feel when I see my clothes on a catwalk. That will never go away. I love being able to create aesthetic environments and create clothes that change the very atmosphere of an environment. I could say the greatest times are when I open a new account or secure a very high-profile client, but, in truth, I enjoy most the simplicity of transforming a metre of fabric into a garment that somebody feels really good in and adores wearing.

BRIAN LONG

Co-founder and CEO, Parthus

In just eight years, Brian Long has created a major Irish multinational company that has become a leader in its field. Parthus is one of the largest intellectual property companies in the world. It employs over 300 of the world's most highly skilled semiconductor design engineers yet does not manufacture any tangible products. Parthus retains the intellectual property rights to the designs of semiconductor chips that power the mobile Internet and licenses this knowledge to equipment manufacturers and leading semiconductor companies. At a time when technology companies are being ruined by stock market volatility, Parthus's licensing business model continues to win the favour of investors. When Parthus conducted an initial public offering in May 2000, its share price soared 66% on the first day of trading to value the company at over £1 billion and Brian Long's own remaining 23% stake at almost £250 million. Just over three months later, the price had rocketed to five times its offering value. Although the share price has since dropped from such dizzying heights, Parthus has consistently posted record results since its flotation. Parthus's technology changes fundamentally the way individuals communicate and use the Internet. It gives people the freedom to converse and send data across the world without recourse to fixed-line connections. It delivers location awareness to a user anywhere on the planet, pinpointing lost children, stolen cars or emergency victims. It makes possible instantaneous down-

loading of data and music from the Internet to a mobile handheld device and enables voice recognition and command. Brian Long's enterprise is changing the world in which we live.

<hr />

Young enterprise

I am originally from Swords in Co. Dublin, but my family of seven moved to Whitehall when I was young. I attended O'Connell's School in Dublin's city centre as my father had done before me. From an early age, I became interested in technical gadgets. I joined the school electronics club and found myself engrossed in making little circuits and amplifiers and radio sets. Making electronic circuits became a forte and something that interested me much more than the usual academic subjects at school. Another great interest of mine as a boy was making money. I was always selling things that people were willing to part with money for. I cultivated a plot for growing and selling vegetables with my brother. I bred and sold guinea pigs and rabbits in our back garden. At one stage, I had eighty animals hopping around the garden, and every child in the neighbourhood had bought a pet from me. I always enjoyed these small, independent enterprise ventures, and I received warm encouragement from my mother, who was herself an independent-minded woman. When we were young, she turned her hand to enterprising activities. Working from home, she edited Leaving and Intermediate Certificate textbooks and revision notes. She also produced books in Irish that did very well. She had a flair for enterprise and was a great influence on me.

When I went to college, I initially studied electronic engineering at the Dublin Institute of Technology on Kevin

Street. I then transferred to Trinity College Dublin and completed a degree in electronics, followed by a master's degree in microelectronics. After completing my postgraduate studies, I spent some time working in the university microelectronic laboratories. My first real job was as a design engineer in Telectron, an Irish telecommunications company. Here I gained real exposure to basic design techniques for telecommunications switches, which was terrific experience. At Telectron I also gained valuable insight into the full spectrum of technology development, comprising design, manufacturing, marketing, sales and shipping. It was a great training ground for me, and I also watched and learnt from several technology companies that had been spun off of Telectron. In my fourth year with the company, Telectron was bought by AT&T. Suddenly, I had exposure to a massive multinational and worked on projects in both Ireland and the United States. After a short interval with a spin-off company called Telspec, a small telecommunications development company, I joined Digital Equipment Corporation (DEC). I worked again in microelectronics and was promoted to head up the analog circuits division. In this position, I learnt a huge amount about the US market. I spent a lot of time on the road trying to win business in the face of fierce competition. While doing business with the large companies that supplied DEC throughout the United States as well as Europe, I established contacts that would become invaluable in later years.

Independent future

At the age of thirty-six, I decided to take control of my own destiny. I had learnt a lot from working in several companies, but I decided it was time to be independent and run my own business. I did not want to start a business that would be a mere offshoot of an existing company – I wanted to create something completely new. It made sense to apply the knowledge of semiconductor chip design that I had acquired over many years. I knew also that chip design was a highly specialized area and that if I could devise new products and services, there would be a high barrier to entry for competitors trying to enter my space. If I could create an exclusive customer base for new chip designs, I would in fact ensure security in an industry that is known for its volatility.

I needed two things to start up a new chip design company – the right employees, who could provide the specialized technology expertise, and customers. I first focussed on getting a good team of people. I was confident that I could find in Ireland the skills and expertise that I needed not only to start up a chip design company but also to meet the future demand for expertise of a growing company. Using the network of contacts I had established during my time in DEC, I hired several people who expressed an interest in working on a design team. I then approached several large semiconductor firms in Europe and the United States with the hope of securing contracts to design silicon chips. One evening, I had dinner in Milan with the senior management of Europe's largest chip manufacturer, the Franco-Italian company STMicroelectronics (ST). I knew they had tremendous expertise in the area of analog technology, and I put it to the management that I could complement this expertise with digital-signal processing skills. I suggested that I could set up a company in Ireland that would design the semiconductor technology they needed and that this would allow them to focus on manufacturing and marketing their chips. I had brought with me a couple of schematics of the kind of chips that we could design, and I convinced the ST executives to come to Ireland to explore further the possibility of a business deal.

Before the ST managers arrived in Dublin, I gathered together a team of designers who had said they would be interested in joining a company if I got it off the ground, and I had several meetings with representatives of Enterprise Ireland. At our first meeting, my assembled potential managers and designers acted as if they were full-time employees and conducted a detailed presentation of how we could create a successful semiconductor chip design business in Ireland. The people from Enterprise Ireland were impressed enough to agree to support us. In effect, we now had the backing of the Irish state and a team of very competent designers and managers, and we could present a very coherent story to the ST managers when they visited. The result was that ST showed an interest in making a deal.

At this point, I met with Peter McManamon, who had excellent experience in financial management and over twelve years' experience in the electronics industry. Peter was a co-founder and director of Videpro International Products Limited, a designer and manufacturer of large-screen projector systems. My engineering background and his accounting and financial background, as well as his business experience, made for a great partnership, and we agreed to write a business plan together. We spent six months perfecting the business plan. We rewrote the plan perhaps twenty times, revising the financials and variables to precision. On the basis of this plan we had repeated negotiations with ST, and they finally agreed to manufacture chips that we would design and for which we would be paid on a rolling, or long-term, contract basis. As part of the deal, ST agreed to provide seed funding in the form of a £300,000 loan that could be converted to stock. Peter and I invested the same amount, and Enterprise Ireland added another £300,000. Enterprise Ireland also provided employment grants, which were an enormous help.

We launched the company in 1993 under the name of Silicon Systems Limited (SSL) and immediately went looking for an end customer that would buy the chips from ST. The first contract we secured was from DEC. I will never forget returning to my old company, explaining that I had started a new company in Ireland that could design chips that another company would manufacture and asking if they would be interested in giving me an order. I was delighted when they agreed. We had won our first contract and would soon see real revenue. The dream of running my own company had become a reality.

Creating respect and stature

We opened our first offices in South Leinster Street in Dublin and went looking for more contracts. We encountered some early barriers to winning business and support. I remember travelling to the United States, sitting in front of a large group of industry experts in Silicon Valley and telling them how we could design chips for them in Ireland. The reaction at the time in the Valley was, 'We invented this stuff, what the hell do you guys in Ireland know? What could you possibly teach us?' I also recall looking for funding from massive US banks that were familiar with the industry in the Valley. They asked, 'Who are these guys from Ireland, and do they really think they have something better to offer?' Today, that attitude has been replaced with a wide respect for our ability and technological expertise, but it served as a good motivator at the time because we worked twice as hard to win a deal.

We won deals to design storage applications and hard-disk drives for DEC, and when DEC was taken over by Quantum

Corporation, we maintained the contracts. Other large corporations, such as Seagate, sought our design expertise, and their custom gave us a tremendous industry vote of confidence. Business spiralled, and we moved into the consumer multimedia world and developed audio systems for the Bose Corporation. Before long, we grew in size to more than 100 employees as we kept winning new contracts and customers. For the first three years, SSL executed the original business plan perfectly. We could not believe how accurately we had planned the business and felt that the early effort was at last justified and that we could scale the business comfortably on a solid foundation.

As SSL grew in stature, we decided that we should bring more industry expertise and distinction to the board of directors. Chairman Michael Pierce, a past president of the Irish Electronics Industry Federation and also the founder and chief executive of the Mentec Group, an Irish company specializing in financial, manufacturing and telecommunication software solutions and imaging technology, added a great deal of credibility. In early 1997, Bill McCabe joined the board as a non-executive director. Bill brought significant experience as chairman of Smartforce plc (formerly CBT Systems plc), an Irish company that has established itself as the largest e-learning company in the world, specializing in interactive educational software. Smartforce had been quoted on the Nasdaq national market since 1995, and Bill's knowledge of taking a firm public would prove invaluable. In 1998 our chief operating officer, Kevin Fielding, joined the board and was soon after made president, in recognition of his key role in the continued growth of the company. The final addition to the board of a non-executive director, Sven-Christer Nilsson, former CEO of Ericsson, has brought balance and international repute to the team.

Our new directors not only invested money of their own

that would help the business grow but also brought new ideas to expand the company at an international level. We agreed that we should look beyond the original business model of self-funding design activities and seek venture capital that would allow us to scale our research and development. In 1997 and 1998, we undertook two rounds of roadshows in the United States to raise funds. We had established a credible presence in America through two offices we had opened there, but it was still daunting to approach such massive financial institutions as Morgan Stanley, Merrill Lynch and Goldman Sachs. Bill McCabe was central in arranging introductions that gave us a positive start. We could show investors that we had a very strong research and development team and world-class product designers and that we had built up an extensive and valuable portfolio of intellectual property in semiconductor design. In December 1998, Goldman Sachs, one of the world's leading global investment banking and securities firms, agreed to invest $16 million in SSL for a 23% stake. This was a watershed for us. Goldman Sachs brought a worldly presence to the company and dramatically increased the number of our global industry contacts and potential customers. The addition of their investment management expertise also helped us with our business strategy and had a positive influence on the future direction of the company.

Revolutionary technology

The $16 million was key in allowing us to build new products. We had the necessary funds to focus on what we believed was the exciting and rewarding area of mobile Internet technology. We saw this technology as the convergence of the cellphone and multimedia applications, and we had a strong base in both. We refocussed on becoming a leading supplier of fully integrated 'platform intellectual property' solutions to manufacturers of next-generation mobile devices. The platform approach develops complete system-on-a-chip solutions for customers looking for market-ready solutions for cost-effective implementation of the new generation of mobile Internet products. In addition, the platform approach greatly reduces customers' time to market, which is of great importance in highly competitive markets.

Our platforms power the mobile Internet, and the range of applications of our designs is very broad. We provide a platform for Bluetooth technology, which enables instant communication between computers, mobile phones and portable handheld organizers. This removes the need for costly and awkward cables. Bluetooth allows a user to surf the Internet and send e-mails via a mobile phone. This market is going to explode. Beyond any doubt, people want mobile phones with data communication capability. When I visit customers in Japan, I can read the *Irish Times* on my mobile phone. I can also check my e-mails, write up the outcome of a meeting and send the information home via the Internet. Bluetooth technology can be applied in everyday devices besides mobile phones. For instance, Agilent, a spin-off of Hewlett–Packard, uses the technology to develop printers that operate without connection cables.

We have designed a platform deployed in a single chip for the Global Positioning System (GPS). GPS processes information from 24 satellites orbiting 11,000 miles above the earth to pinpoint the location of a GPS-enabled device to within 5 metres of accuracy. This technology has breakthrough applications. In the future, all vehicles will have GPS technology that will locate their position and guide them to their destination, highlight traffic jams and find nearby service stations or restaurants. Our GPS platform has been installed in 80,000 lorries and trucks in Switzerland. It monitors their location constantly, detailing when and where they drive on motorways. As a result, tollbooths are no longer necessary, which means that traffic jams no longer occur and motorway control is cheaper. Our GPS platform can also be used to locate instantaneously a caller who dials the emergency services. In fact, the US Federal Communications Commission now requires all mobile phones to carry a GPS chip for this reason. Our GPS chip is so small that it can be placed in a child's watch, allowing parents to locate them using the Internet on their PC or mobile phone. With GPS-enabled phones and taxis, a user can simply enter a request for a taxi in his or her phone, and the closest taxi is pinpointed and hailed to the user's location.

We have also designed a platform for the Internet-audio market. This platform, deployed in a single chip, allows the integration of mobile devices and MP3 technology. MP3 enables digital transfer of music and was developed by the Moving Picture Experts Group. This technology will change the way that music is distributed in the future. For instance, my kids never play a CD at home any more. They log on to the Internet to find and play their favourite music. They have an enormous choice, and the quality is very high. I can install an MP3 player the size of a matchbox on the dashboard of my car and download to my mobile device whatever music I like from the Internet while driving to the beach. It is much more convenient and inexpensive than lugging a CD player and collection of discs around with me.

Our ability to create these platforms for a global market has transformed the company into a global multinational that is one of the world's largest intellectual-property companies and a world-class centre of excellence in semiconductor research and development. We now employ over 300 highly skilled professionals and have grown from our Dublin headquarters to set up sales offices throughout the United States – in San José, San Diego, Chicago, Melbourne, Florida and Austin, Texas – as well as in the United Kingdom, Hong Kong, Japan, Korea, Sweden, Finland, Germany and France. We have eight development centres located in Ireland (Dublin, Cork, Limerick and Belfast), the United States (San José, California, and Melbourne, Florida), the United Kingdom (Northampton) and France (Caen). Our customers are some of the world's largest semiconductor companies and equipment manufacturers, including 3Com, Microsoft, Motorola, ARM Holdings, Psion, STMicroelectronics, Texas Instruments and Agilent.

Going public

The growth of the company has been phenomenal, but the most exciting event for me was our initial public offering (IPO) in May 2000. A flotation of company stock would raise sufficient funds to allow us to expand aggressively our research and development capability and make strategic acquisitions. The IPO was also a very important stage in the cultivation of our international image because of the huge publicity that accompanies a flotation. We decided that it would be an opportune time to rebrand the company. Silicon Systems Limited was not only something of a tongue-twister but was also a difficult name to register in several countries where other companies had adopted it. A marketing team brainstormed ideas for a new name and eventually recommended 'Parthus', a word with Greek roots that implies bringing different parts together, or integration, and a name I was happy to have as a title for the company.

Goldman Sachs agreed to act as global co-ordinator, book-runner and sponsor of the public offering, and a consortium of banks consisting of Chase Hambrecht & Quist, Donaldson, Lufkin & Jenrette and Lehman Brothers assisted Goldman as co-lead managers for the fund-raising. It was decided that Parthus would be launched on both the London Stock Exchange and the US Nasdaq exchange. Once again, I left Dublin with a team of managers for an intensive roadshow. The roadshow team went on the trail for two and a half weeks, jumping from city to city, meeting investors and drumming up interest for the impending launch. It was terrific and exciting. It was stimulating to be talking to a potential investor on the West Coast of the United States and then meeting another potential investor the next day in Japan. I found it very interesting to experience so many differences in culture and in accepted ways of conducting business across geographical boundaries in such a short space of time. It was also very tiring and stressful. I had grown accustomed to travelling long distances over many years, but the intensity of the roadshow and the importance of the meetings and presentations caught up with me. Despite the stress, I ultimately felt that if I was not part of the action, I would be bored.

Several factors contributed to a very high investor interest in Parthus. We had a business model that investors loved. We give other companies the option of avoiding fixed costs in research and development and manufacturing by allowing them to license design technology from us. This works extremely well in a tight market because we do not have large sunk costs ourselves. Royalty revenues go straight to our bottom line in our income statement and are not affected by the cost of goods manufactured. In effect, we have a 100% gross margin, which the stock market loves. We generate a rich revenue stream by imposing a licence fee in the region of $1 million as soon as a customer agrees to adopt a Parthus technology. Furthermore, Parthus is paid an additional royalty of approximately 5% of the price of a chip every time a product is sold to an end-user. In the weeks before the IPO, we signed a deal with British company ARM Holdings in which ARM took a $2 million equity stake in Parthus and agreed to allow Parthus to license ARM's core technology to our clients. ARM is the Intel of mobile phones, and the deal was seen as a further vote of confidence by potential investors.

On the last day of the roadshow, we fixed the share price offering at 85p sterling and $12.60 per American depository share (ADS), with each ADS representing ten ordinary shares. Mid-2000 was a disastrous time for technology share prices, as the shakeout was under full steam and many reputable global technology firms were faltering in the stock market. Nonetheless, our roadshow experience had made us confident of a successful launch, and we went to the market with 130 million shares, or 23% of the company, on Friday, 19 May 2000. It was a phenomenally successful IPO. The shares were oversubscribed 35 times with a 60–40 split between European and US investors. At the end of the first day of trading, the value of the shares had jumped 66% from their placing price. At the market closing in London, Parthus was valued at £765 million sterling, or just over £1 billion in Irish punts. We had become one of the biggest Irish enterprises and a formidable multinational company.

Things went from good to better in the following months. We announced an increase in revenues of 57% for the first six months of 2000 and made significant developments in our

Bluetooth platform that allowed the technology to be incorporated into mobile phones. ARM agreed to incorporate our platform in its manufactured chips, which are carried in 50% of the world's mobile phones. In early September, the Parthus share price jumped to an unprecedented level of 419p sterling, almost five times the initial offering price. While the price would fall again in subsequent months, it was a strong indication of shareholders' confidence in our future growth.

We embarked on an investigation of potential acquisition targets that would strengthen our position in the third-generation mobile telephony and Internet infrastructure software markets. Although we had $135 million in cash reserves, we considered making a second offering of shares on the stock market to increase our reserve and widen the scope of possible acquisitions. On 12 November 2000, Parthus raised an additional £15.5 million sterling from the sale of over 8 million shares. Existing shareholders, including Goldman Sachs, Enterprise Ireland, venture capital firm Kelburn and Parthus executives also sold shares worth some £98 million to new investors.

A bright future

We closed 2000 very positively by recording an increase of 77% in sales for the year. Sales increases in 2001 will again be strong – approximately 60% – and we intend to break even and start to record profits in 2002. The future is bright for Parthus. Even at a time when technology companies continue to take a battering in the volatile stock market, Parthus is reporting record earnings. We are protected by the fact that companies maintain spending in research and development to guarantee future products and revenues. Even in a long-term recession scenario, consumers will still want more functionality on their mobile phones. The technology that we provide is not going to go away. We have also diversified enough not to be completely exposed to a downturn in one area of technology. As well as our major presence in enabling the mobile Internet, we also provide navigational and voice-recognition technology, and even gaming technology for the Microsoft X-Box, which is set to become a huge product. Parthus has $160 million on its balance sheet and can afford to embark on a series of mergers and acquisitions that will strengthen its position in the years ahead.

My goal for Parthus is to manage its phenomenal growth carefully and to ensure that it continues to exceed the expectations of the marketplace as it has since the IPO. I want to see Parthus leverage its business model. Five of the top ten semiconductor companies in the world license our technology, and we are aiming to make that ten out of ten. Dataquest has ranked Parthus as the fifth-largest intellectual-property developer in the world by revenue, and I believe we will be number one in three years. We have established a critical mass that is extremely hard to emulate, and with the best design engineers in the world in Ireland, Parthus will be a very hard company to beat.

Latent Irish energy

The abundance of internationally successful Irish high-tech companies is something that was waiting to happen. Ten years ago, Ireland had a latent energy that was ready to come to the surface. The country has never before had the level of entrepreneurship that has recently surfaced. In the past, young Irish people who emigrated to the United States achieved wonderful success there, and we were left asking the question, 'What was wrong that they did not want to stay in Ireland?' A major change that I think has encouraged young people to stay in Ireland and create a successful living is the increase in the level of education and skills. Not long ago, the country had only three schools of engineering. Now, countless technology courses in regional technical colleges and universities throughout the country produce a highly educated and motivated young workforce. A second ingredient that has contributed to the success of Irish high-tech companies is the availability of venture capital. At one time, Irish investors were terrified of technology, and there was very little risk money in Ireland. Through some early high-tech successes that Enterprise Ireland helped to foster, US venture capital began to trickle into Ireland. With more Irish success stories such as CBT, Trintech and IONA Technologies, the focus of venture capital investors became more intense, and Ireland soon established itself as a world centre for software, information and communications technology. It is perceived as an excellent base for smart investment with good people.

The work rate of Irish people today is also much greater than a decade ago. People choose to work harder because the opportunities and rewards are enormous. Irish people are improving their lifestyle and standards of living. Many Irish people are securing enormous newly found wealth. When people acquire large amounts of money, they are initially shocked. Ultimately, it becomes a very acceptable fact, and people get on with their life and work on a day-to-day basis. In my own case, I have been able to clear my mortgage, eliminate the stress of financial worries and take nicer holidays. After that, it is good to have the ability to help other people when necessary. Beyond a slight improvement in quality of life, there is very little difference. I am not interested in buying things that I do not really need – why have three cars if I only need one?

There is a price that is paid for the opportunities to work

harder and make more money – we have fewer hours of personal freedom and more congested cities. However, I do not think that Irish people will ever forget how to enjoy themselves. Although they work hard, they know how to play hard too. A young engineer in his early thirties returned from Silicon Valley recently to look for a job in Ireland. When I asked him why he wanted to return from the Valley, he said that the work was as exciting in Ireland and that the Valley did not have the enjoyable lifestyle he could find at home. He believed that the balance was just right in Ireland.

The thing I enjoy most when I reflect on the success of Parthus is the thought that we have made the company grow from a small technology start-up into a major multinational player of international repute. I get a big kick when I consider the engineers and managers who started with the company and have achieved a level of financial comfort that they are happy with. They took a big risk at the outset and now no longer have to beg for a mortgage or apply for a bank loan to buy a car. It is nice to see young families for whom financial troubles are a thing of the past. I also love the idea that we have put another Irish technology company on the world map, competing with the biggest companies in the world, and winning.

BARRY McDONAGH

Founder, thegoodspider.com website

*B*arry McDonagh has achieved a sense of personal contentment that comes from his commitment to live his life according to his beliefs, regardless of convention. After graduating with an arts degree from University College Dublin, he might well have succumbed to the security and comfort that his first, tourism-related job offered. However, belief in the revolutionary potential of new communications technology compelled him to pass on security. Barry believes that the power of the Internet, in particular, is most meaningfully applied in the creation of a sense of community. And a sense of community, he believes, is the bedrock of a society in which he would like to live. His enterprise and imagination, are founded on these beliefs.

Barry conceived and then developed the imaginative thegoodspider.com website. The site is an Internet portal that acts as a gateway to the Web through a choice selection of search engines. Every time the website is visited, at no expense to the user, the advertisers on the site accumulate a fee to be paid to the Third World development agency Concern. The growing number of people who set thegoodspider.com as their default homepage share a common desire to achieve a positive impact on poverty. Through this shared purpose, they enlist willingly in a community. Thegoodspider.com has garnered Barry attention and respect in the Internet industry. In December 2000, he was awarded the Irish Internet Association's annual Net Visionary award in recognition of the contribution he has made to the *development and promotion of the Internet industry in Ireland and beyond.*

Working on something he believes in has unleashed his personal energy and creativity. This in turn fuels his determination to ensure the international success and proliferation of the site. He embraces liberal values such as freedom of choice and the empowerment of the individual as a force for change, yet he subscribes also to strong traditional ideas of family and societal order. He sees no conflict in doing so. Instead, he feels that modern and traditional values can complement each other constructively and that his generation has the confidence, the ability and the modern tools to reconcile these supposedly incompatible values.

The blue-eyed 24-year-old and I met in a sun-drenched garden recess opposite the National Concert Hall in Dublin. Surrounded by glassy office buildings, I listened to his articulate and easy-going chat.

My generation

There is definitely a unique new spirit alive in the young people of my generation. To some extent, it is a natural and inherent youthful hope, but more importantly, it is a new confidence in people who do not know the fear of failing. Some years ago, I spent a summer with a group of student friends working in the United States. Each of us came home with a new attitude: If you start something new but fail, then that is a positive experience. Traditionally in Ireland, it has been quite daunting to fail. There is a heavy stigma associated with failure, as if it points to a blemish of character. Now this attitude has been discarded very swiftly in favour of one that promotes every experience as a good one. I have also enjoyed spending time studying and teaching in Germany and Spain. In comparison with young people in both countries, I feel that young Irish people have less fear of failure and a stronger spirit and eagerness to 'have a go' at starting a new company or enterprise initiative.

My generation has the availability of new tools. Realizing the potential of the Internet is the epitome of starting something new and fresh. Young people have great confidence in harnessing the Internet because they know that they are the first to do so. Nobody can claim to have twenty years' experience with the Internet, so the pitch is effectively level for us all. Young people have a more comfortable grasp of the usefulness of the Internet than older generations. It should not necessarily be so, but the established, grey-suited professionals tend to create mental blocks. They do not yet fully appreciate the power and reach of the Internet in a meaningful way.

Internet fascination

I studied German and archaeology for three years at UCD. I enjoyed my studies, but throughout that time, I felt a slow-burning, smouldering interest in the Internet grow into something I simply could not resist. In fact, I endured something of a struggle in my final year to maintain a healthy interest in my degree studies. The Internet is pure fascination. I am mentally blown away by it. I find it more and more interesting the closer I look at its infrastructure. As a kid, I had a sense of wonder about the ability of a fax machine to send a picture. The Internet increased that wonder with its multidimensional nature. I started using a program called Instant Messenger that transmitted a sentence to another remotely connected user as I typed. The speed at which that information travels any distance across the Internet is incredible. Time and space collapse. As with many people, I have educated myself about the Internet. There is a wealth of information from online tutorials that inexpensively surpasses what you might learn in a class. The inclination to work on an Internet-related project grew stronger and overtook any ambition I had to work in archaeology in Ireland. I had spent some time working as a guide in Dublin Castle and Government Buildings but was not very excited about this work. Archaeological work in Ireland has the tendency to be cold and wet, so working on the Internet literally had the appeal of greater warmth.

The good spider

In 1999 I was watching the Net Aid concert, a charity concert to raise funds for projects in developing countries that was broadcast simultaneously from New York and London on both the television and the Internet. At one point in the proceedings, David Bowie was interviewed. He talked about the potential of using the collective wealth of knowledge of the many people who used his own Internet service provider (ISP). I started to play with the thought of attracting a large number of people to a website and using their attention for a collective purpose. In particular, I thought about the possibilities that the Internet offered to constructively build a shared sense of community among those who used it.

I did some research and found the US website called the Hunger Site. At this site, people can register and donate funds directly to several different charities that provide food relief in developing countries. The site is visited over 220,000 times a day, and since its inception in June 1999, over 100 million people have made donations through the site, creating a phenomenal sense of collective action. I liked this concept of a site making a worthwhile contribution and decided to create a site that contributed to the Irish charity Concern. I visited managers in Concern and chatted with them about the concept. They immediately liked the idea and wanted to help develop it. I had hoped that Concern would have some in-house expertise or resources devoted to website development that I could use, but they had none at all. Concern offered to take me on as an employee so that I could support myself and develop the site with them at the same time. I felt that this was perfect. I could belong to an organization with a strong purpose, make enough to get by and work on a project that fuelled my interest. In a way, the move was a very natural progression for me. I had always wanted to create something from nothing in a businesslike way. Several business ideas had seeded, grown and withered in my mind, but here at last was an initiative that grabbed my interest and in which I believed. At Concern, I created thegoodspider.com as a portal that people can log on to and from which they can seek direction to any point in the Web, using search engines. As a selective search-engine facility, thegoodspider.com is unlike other charitable websites. We decided to use a creative name that we felt was fun and that referred to the other name for the Internet: the World Wide Web. A website name is the only address contact to the world, so it has to be easy to remember and spell. Most generic names such as 'food.com' had been reserved. Nonetheless, thegoodspider.com seemed just as memorable.

When I joined Concern, we agreed on a deadline of two months to set up the website. A schoolfriend of mine, Keith O'Toole, worked voluntarily on the design of the site and I set out to persuade companies to advertise on the site. It is often said that building Internet sites is a costly affair. In truth, we managed to set up the website with no third-party financial backing, using only our shared knowledge and time. Overheads and maintenance costs are low, and the revenue generation mechanism is very simple. Each company pays for a user's viewing of their advertisements. The companies buy blocks of hits – the occasions on which a user sees their advertisements. When they achieve 100,000 hits, I bill them. The £1,500 that they pay for each block goes directly to Concern, which spends it on foodstuffs in the Third World. Every single hit raises enough advertising revenue to provide one simple meal. People can set thegoodspider.com to be the default homepage that opens each time they access the Internet. When users enter our website, they are making a conscious choice to conduct a search of the Web through thegoodspider.com, knowing that as a result, money will be donated to Concern. In this way, they share a collective purpose.

I believed strongly in the concept from the outset. I would not continue to work with it now unless I believed it was going to have a very big effect. The Irish launch in June 2000, in Dublin Castle, went very well. The number of people who helped voluntarily surprised me. Family, friends and associates alike gave tremendous help and support. The positive coverage in the national newspapers was a very encouraging start. The growth in the number of people visiting the site has been exponential. Some 3,800 people visited the site in its first month of operation, some 25,000 in its third month and some 70,000 in its sixth month. A year after it first launched, the site had over 150,000 hits a month. The next step is to expand the site by aiming at the huge UK audience.

That the site has grown so explosively is due to an effect

called 'viral marketing'. People spread the concept of the website by word of mouth and through their individual e-mail networks. Positive 'word of mouth' – in this case by way of e-mail – proves to be the most coveted form of marketing, yet is very difficult to create. One person might dart an e-mail about thegoodspider.com to their list of e-mail contacts. Within minutes, there will be a surge of perhaps fifty people who like the idea and immediately set the site as their homepage. This type of advertising is incredibly fast and powerful. In January 2001, in the aftermath of the serious earthquake in India, Concern sent a single e-mail to 2,000 regular donors and received a phenomenal response within hours. Compared with traditional methods of raising awareness, the efficiency in terms of time, human resources, printing and administration of one click of a button is huge. Charitable organizations have been realizing the value of the Internet only very recently. Online volunteering, live news feeds and e-mail petitions are contributing to the growing strength of non-profit organizations. The Jubilee 2000 campaign, which strove to remove debt in the developing world, could not have been co-ordinated on such an ambitiously worldwide scale without the ease of mass communication that the Internet allows.

We are learning that users of the Internet prefer not to surf haphazardly any more. They are far more discerning about how they spend their time online. The chaotic amount of online information that users must deal with drives their online attention to the safe havens of websites with which they feel a natural affinity. This growing trend leaves Ireland and Irish people at an advantage, given the global spread and number of people who claim some form of Irish ancestry. It is this factor that has made many Irish Internet enterprises successful and profitable.

The scattered Irish diaspora and viral marketing have increased the awareness of thegoodspider.com to far-flung countries of the world where Irish expatriates and associates have heard of the site from their friends at home. People log on from the Far East, Australia, South Africa, the United States, Latin America and across Europe every morning. They are comfortable using the Internet as an Irish touchstone and show a strong preference for donating to an Irish-based charity over a charity in their own country of residence that would likely carry out similar aid work. The expansion of this community is wonderful, but it does pose an interesting advertising anomaly. Some companies that want to advertise on our site are excited by the growing number of hits that we are receiving, but when they see the diverse geographic profile of users, they realize that the message to a local target market is diluted. The biggest markets in Ireland are office workers who surf at break times and students who have a natural affinity with the Internet. The effect of office Internet use is very apparent in the fivefold reduction in hits recorded at weekends. Student users are an ideal target market both for thegoodspider.com and advertisers such as banks. Banks are eager to win the allegiance of potential customers who are at an age just prior to wage-earning, and thegoodspider.com benefits from the idealism and philanthropic attitude of students who may not have sufficient funds to donate directly.

Shaping the Internet

Advertising on the Internet in general is going through a lot of change. For several years, established companies were slow to engage in online advertising. They preferred to hold onto the traditional model for advertising. Then there was a shift in

Charlie Ardagh

Photograph courtesy of Frank Fennell

Moya Doherty

Chris Horn

Eddie Jordan

Louise Kennedy

Brian Long

Barry McDonagh

Cyril McGuire

thinking that concluded that while the billboard was more tangible, it did not necessarily yield a greater return on investment. However, Internet advertising remains something of an experiment for many companies. The rate at which Internet users are actually 'clicking through' an advert to reach the site of an advertiser has fallen dramatically to a mere 0.5%. Different Internet sites are adopting novel ways to overcome this and entice users to click on the advertising banners. For example, some advertisers associate prizes such as holidays with their banners. Thegoodspider.com has introduced a concept of advertising that assures a visitor that if they actually click through to the site of an advertiser, this will be recorded, and the advertiser will donate two extra meals of grain. It is up to the advertiser, of course, to convert the higher click-through rate into actual custom.

Many established companies have a fear of the unknown in relation to the Internet. In response to the pressure to create an Internet presence quickly, they contract Web designers to perform what they imagine to be a highly technical and complex process of website design and construction. In fact, a good-quality and functioning website can be built in an afternoon. Once a few basic tricks for constructing a site have been learnt, it is a relatively simple operation. Standard software packages facilitate the design and construction of a website by removing the need to hand-type computer code, such that it becomes little more than a cut and paste exercise. There has been an explosive growth in website design companies that make a living from the fear of the unknown and help established companies to make the 'bricks to clicks' transition. While the mystery can be taken out of the construction, great skill and artistry still reside in the work of graphic designers. Their creative input makes an enormous difference to the attractiveness of a website.

The Internet is not fully established, but it has found a certain mould. I am disappointed with and disillusioned by that mould. The nature of the Internet now plays a part in isolating us as individual users. We are isolated at one terminal, often in a one-to-one dialogue with characterless retail entities selling products and services to us. At the other end of the spectrum to the individual user, some of those involved in building the Internet are creating dotcom companies with a view to generating personal fortunes rather than ensuring that the greatest user benefit is derived from the Internet. Despite the dotcom shakeout, newspapers continue to dedicate pages to the newest e-commerce players and focus on venture capital investments and possible flotations. There is a real risk that the Internet is set to become as passive as television, a medium in which the only sites worth visiting are the ones offering the cheapest deal, the most amazing sale or the craziest entertainment. In fifteen years, people may turn around and rue their failure to realize the potential of this powerful entity. There is more to the Internet than the chaos of a virtual shopping mall.

I believe that the Internet can be used to empower, not isolate, the individual. Thegoodspider.com is about bringing people together on one page as a community. By the power and unity of numbers, we can make a change to people's lives. For the launch of the site, we used the Irish slogan 'Níl neart gan chur le chéile': 'There's no strength without unity.'

Internet freedom

I also believe that the Internet should be given the freedom to develop without the constraint of censorship. From its inception, the concept of the Internet has always revolved around openness and transparency of information. The Internet is an honest reflection of the human state. A search engine cannot tell a lie. Typing any bizarre idea into a search field will inevitably result in a connection to a site that matches the idea. Bizarre ideas and pornography are natural elements of a universal human psyche and as such are reflected on the Internet. Censoring the content of the Internet is like blocking out parts of human psychology and the human condition and ignoring their existence. A collection of individuals will ultimately find a sensible level of self-regulation that ensures the importance of freedom of communication without online anarchy. The Internet is a tool that is no better or worse than the people who use it.

The struggle between Napster and the established music industry is an example of one aspect of censorship of the Internet. Napster is a simple file-sharing program created by a college student, Brian Fannin. At the Napster website, visitors could download music files directly from other people's personal computer hard drives and transfer them across the Internet to their own hard drives. This file-sharing bypasses the conventional music retail channels. Less than five months after its release, the popularity of the Napster software threatened the future of the entire music industry. Bands such as Metallica and the Corrs openly condemned it, and the record companies that stood to lose royalties as a consequence of Napster laid siege to its right to operate on the Internet. The resultant censorship of file-sharing through the Napster site was fully in favour of the record companies but a regressive step for the freedom of the Internet. The Internet will undoubtedly be the biggest medium for music transfer in the future, so both sides will ultimately have to work out a more balanced compromise in order to work together and co-exist. This episode marks the culmination of the first stage of maturity of the Internet in its short lifetime. It marks a greater climax than the pinnacle achieved by dotcoms before the shakeout: the fact that a simple file-sharing program developed by a student could cause such upheaval gives a taste of the power of communal sharing on the Internet that has yet to come.

Information and absolute poverty

The Internet is a radically new source of information and knowledge. Those who have access can use this information and knowledge to their benefit. Those who do not have access or who choose to ignore the medium will be less well off by comparison. This may be seen as a new poverty – information poverty. Interestingly, the modern working class in Ireland has a thirst for information. Provision of computers in homes, schools and libraries is quenching the thirst for information and knowledge and giving rise to Internet enterprise activities. Education expense and social prejudice are lesser constraints for people who have access to the flow of unrestricted information on the Internet. In this way the Internet has a social levelling effect. Any individual can harness and apply this new source of knowledge. Developing countries are less fortunate. The lack of infrastructure for computing and communication means that access to information is a lower priority than basic survival needs such as access to water, food and shelter. Information poverty will, for some time, widen the gap between developed and developing countries.

Concern is an association of people with a collective purpose, which is to assist people in the least developed countries of the world. The agency began more than thirty years ago in response to the famine in Biafra (now part of Nigeria) in 1968. Today, 2,500 Concern volunteers work in nineteen of the world's least developed countries, mainly in Africa and Asia, endeavouring to eliminate absolute poverty. Poverty restricts people's choices – not their competence or abilities. Concern maintains a respect for the integrity of people who cannot help themselves as a result of their choice-shackling conditions and environment. Development is not a handout or a gift that can be given to people. It is a process that occurs in people, through their own capacity and at their own pace. Concern tries to facilitate self-development based on the inherent skills and local resources that people living in absolute poverty possess.

Concern approaches the elimination of absolute poverty in three ways: emergency response; development work; and development education and advocacy work. Emergency response is the most visible part of Concern's work. It involves a reactive response to natural disasters such as floods, earthquakes, cyclones and droughts, as well as political or man-made disasters such as civil war. The difference between emergency response and development work is similar to the difference between giving someone a fish and teaching someone how to fish. Although relief is needed in emergencies, human dignity requires that people be able to rely on their own work to survive. Concern spends almost half of its resources on programmes that help people to use resources more efficiently and earn more in order to assert their right to food, shelter, health and education services. Development work includes programmes promoting rural and urban development, health care, general and HIV education, and credit and savings schemes. Development education and advocacy work aims to facilitate the withdrawal in the First World of policies that make it difficult for less developed countries to compete against developed countries. Some 5% of Concern's resources is devoted to influencing public opinion and policy-makers so that policies in richer countries are just and progressive. Issues such as international debt and militarization are at the top of Concern's agenda.

If it is not creative, it's dead

I am really enjoying working on the site for Concern. It has opened up a whole creative area in my own life. I am spending time with different organizations to think up new ways in which they can use the Internet. If what I do is creative, I enjoy it. If it is not creative, it's dead. I work in a place that has a purpose. I have tried working in the secure environments of large companies but found little sense of purpose, morale or dedication to a common goal. With Concern, I am working on what is important to me. I will spend two years totally dedicated to this work. My whole motivation is to establish thegoodspider.com very strongly throughout Europe. I believe that we can widen the sense of community that thegoodspider.com has created across national borders and cultures. On the website, we have introduced a map of the world that displays graphically the locations of people around the world who have made thegoodspider.com their homepage.

After I have strengthened the site's presence in Europe, I will pull back and allow other people in Concern to take the responsibility. I do not have a long-term career mapped out. Other charities have asked me to set up similar sites for them, but that would be impossible. I cannot do the same thing twice. I have a growing desire to vent new creative ideas. I have picked up my guitar again and like to play music gigs with friends at the weekends and could easily enjoy a life on the road for some time. An acting career is something that also holds an appeal for me. I do not have to make decisions now, and when the time comes to choose, I will know what is right for me. This is a new freedom that my generation shares for the first time. This freedom is an abundance of opportunity that makes the future wide open to us all.

Freedom and choice

Freedom is a curious asset. Freedom is to be embraced, but there are some downsides to the luxurious freedom of choice. One shortcoming is a subtle corrosion of character. In the world of virtual working and virtual careers, people are taking on a new type of flexibility that they call freedom. The old sense of flexibility meant adapting to changing circumstances without losing one's essential shape, like a tree that bends in the wind but returns to a standing position. Now flexibility means changing swiftly from one shape to the next in constant flux – having no true shape at all. Modern flexibility means having fewer attachments and being somewhat adrift. Is this freedom?

The dissatisfaction that this can invoke is clear around any café or pub table. People wonder what others are doing, what their next move is, if others are doing better than they themselves are. You may say that dissatisfaction is a human instinct that stretches us to higher achievements, but the lack of contentment is affecting family structures. People are waiting much longer to raise a family, and kids are losing out. Children should always have a parent at home, whether it is a man or a woman. It sounds old-fashioned, but children ten years behind me experience a sense of abandonment and lack of attention that will affect the balance of their future lives. I was never too enamoured of the figurehead status and special aura that religious leaders assumed, but the demise of religion means that people are losing something. We are focussed on the immediate world around us, but when we go home, where is the spirituality? I think we are going to reach a crisis point in our lifetime when people realize that extreme individualism does not work in a society.

Another aspect of this new freedom of choice is that Irish people now choose not to work in certain positions that they feel are beneath them. Jobs in supermarkets and fast food restaurants are being left to foreign nationals. I was born in Dublin but throughout my school years spent four months each year in a small town called Tina in Co. Galway. I preferred the space of the countryside but did love Galway city and still feel a strong connection with it. A year ago, I watched the Macnas parade at the Galway Arts Festival. It featured animations of vividly coloured exotic birds under siege by local black crows. It was a lot of colourful fun but was intended to reflect something of the current attitude to diversity in Ireland. We have so much to gain from diverse cultures, but we choose not to.

All these things contribute to the erosion of community in Ireland. By bringing people together for a common purpose and by sharing diverse ideas, we can help to shape our community. I think the Internet has a role to play in shaping the community of the future, and I think my generation has the opportunity to fulfil that potential.

CYRIL McGUIRE

Co-founder and executive chairman, Trintech Group plc

*T*he character of a company often reflects that of its
founders. This is especially true of Trintech, the Irish-
based electronic-payment software company that employs
more than 650 people on 4 continents, with global customers
in more than 30 countries. Trintech is strongly associated with
its founding brothers, Cyril and John McGuire, who launched
the company in 1987. I met Cyril McGuire at Trintech
headquarters, overlooking the Leopardstown racecourse, in
south Co. Dublin. The ultra-modern headquarters has a
serious, clinical and clean feel. In contrast to the workforces at
other software companies I have visited, the smartly suited staff
assume a formal and busy air and do not gather for casual chat.
Security is high for personnel and visitors alike, and every piece
of furniture is in its place. An enormous hand-stitched tapestry,
personally chosen by Cyril McGuire, presides over the airy
lobby and defines the ambience. Cyril himself brims with
confidence as he points out the achievements that Trintech has
made in its relatively short existence.

I realize that everything is as it should be. The serious
atmosphere, the formality and the confidence are elements of
a necessary culture, what Cyril calls an 'inherent fabric', in a
company that is the world's largest provider of secure-
payment software.

Trintech has let its hair down on occasion. Its software
authorized the world's first electronic transaction in the new

European single currency on the stroke of midnight, 1 January 1999 – appropriately, with the purchase of a bottle of champagne.

Trintech made one of the most highly publicized international stock market flotations of an Irish company in recent years. In September 1999 its initial share price offering on the Nasdaq exchange was a little over $11. Less than six months later, the share price had, remarkably, increased almost sevenfold to top $75, netting the McGuire brothers a paper value of over $300 million each. In October 1999, the Irish Software Association awarded Trintech the Software Company of the Year award, while Cyril McGuire won the Ernst & Young/Business & Finance Entrepreneur of the Year award. Presenting him with the prize, John Hogan, managing partner of Ernst & Young, said, 'Cyril McGuire exemplifies the way Irish entrepreneurs have been able to develop and sustain successful businesses in the fast-moving world of technology.' Trintech and the McGuire brothers have become pace-setters in the Irish enterprise world. It is their precedent that a multitude of subsequent Irish start-ups seek to follow. Trintech has not escaped technology stock volatility since its heady stock market pinnacle, but its future growth is assured if Cyril McGuire realizes his ambitions for the company.

<hr />

Foundations

Let's be clear, if I had not launched into business with Trintech, I would have found another way into enterprise. I am not the type of person who would be happy with a comfortable, pensionable job. My whole family is quite entrepreneurial. Several of my brothers had set up successful businesses in Connacht, so there was a healthy peer pressure to follow suit. It was always a case of when rather than if I would go into business.

I laid a solid foundation with a good commerce degree at University College Dublin and then built on that knowledge with a master's degree in business, also at UCD. In my MBS, I specialized in finance and marketing, my two strongest subjects. The most valuable lesson I took from my studies was the ability and confidence to approach business problems within a logical framework. After my studies, I joined an established bank, the Industrial Credit Corporation plc (ICC). I entered ICC on the basis that I would learn as much as I could in three or four years. In the end, I gave it four and a half years and enjoyed it tremendously.

I was fortunate to secure the job of heading up the high-tech investment centre at ICC, where my responsibilities included the appraisal of electronic industry investment projects. I became comfortable with the concept of undertaking the risk associated with an investment. Although the majority of investments worked out well, some did not, so I got a taste of the consequences of risk. Having always intended to start my own business, I set about learning everything I could about the indigenous and multinational high-tech companies that ICC worked with. I wanted to learn everything about these companies in terms of their structures, information flows, communications, human relations and operations. It was a terrific experience. I learnt as much through a process of osmosis as through direct observation. The banking background also gave me a tremendous confidence in dealing with bankers and understanding the way in which they think and act. I also learnt the basic criteria for lending and investing – an invaluable insight for future business activities.

Trintech

During my time at ICC, my brother John was doing his engineering dissertation at Trinity College Dublin. He was very keen to research technology that had a commercial application. He devised an ingenious method of sending credit card numbers through radio subcarrier waves when they are used in a transaction at the point of sale. This method could be applied to stop fraudulent use of stolen credit cards. His concept won the Hewlett–Packard award for innovation in electronics in his final year at Trinity College. This technology gave us the platform we had waited for to launch a commercial venture. While John developed the technology, I wrote a business plan. We approached Forbairt (now Enterprise Ireland), the state body charged with fostering the development of indigenous industry, and managed to secure a grant of £150,000. We obtained another £350,000 in several trade board grants and venture capital. I left the shelter of ICC in 1987 to start Trintech with John and an initial workforce of less than five. It was a humble beginning.

We believed absolutely in Trintech from its inception. We were very confident, and it was merely a question of how successful we would be – would we achieve a lucrative trade sale of the company or achieve the ultimate goal of a stock market flotation? In fact, we were more than confident; we had a passion and a hunger. We would not be where we are today if we did not have a genuine, instinctive desire to win, a desire to create and to build something with a life of its own. This attitude pervades the company.

Trintech is a success story in an industry going through profound growth. Electronic commerce is the biggest revolution in Internet technology, and Trintech has products that are absolutely essential to make electronic commerce work. Put simply, payment goes to the heart of commerce – there is no commerce without payment. Our products are not an optional extra – they are a fundamental necessity for successful and secure e-commerce. The market in which we sell is extremely large and growing rapidly. Our management share our passion and hunger to win in that market, and if the Internet has taught us anything, it is that the winner takes all.

People say to me that I am Trintech, but though I may have a hand on the wheel, it has ultimately been the collective effort of everyone in the company that has enabled us to achieve what we have. There are some 15 people that have been a part of Trintech since the beginning, and our workforce has now risen to over 400. About one-quarter of the workforce are now millionaires on paper. That they have realized the fruits of their labour is great. I would like nothing more than to make every staff member a millionaire, something I believe is fully achievable. Commitment and leadership can achieve such success, but clearly, there is an associated significant risk.

First-mover growth

Trintech is a company that has grown up with the electronic payments business since its inception. At the beginning, the company developed payment software for off-line credit card transactions at the point of sale. From point-of-sale card systems software, Trintech progressed to providing payment applications for airline reservations systems operated by the world's largest carriers. This gave us a unique insight into the payment requirements of large international businesses.

We started to develop a range of software products that harnessed the power of the new global medium of information exchange – the Internet. Moving into Internet payment software was a huge challenge and an opportunity for Trintech. The challenge was to build a range of Internet payment products that were robust, secure and easy to install on a global basis. The opportunity lay in the open nature of the Internet. Trintech participated in the formation and implementation of the secure electronic transaction (SET) electronic commerce specifications. In this way, we entered the industry on the ground floor. We helped to bring a set of accepted standards to the way that Internet purchases are made, and that enabled us to offer standard Internet products to a customer base around the world.

As Trintech moved into the global market, we seeded new locations in new countries with Irish 'emissaries of enterprise'. Irish staff would locate in a foreign country and build up the fabric of a new organization. They would then recruit local staff and instil the company culture. Five people travelled to Frankfurt to set up our German operations. Now we have fifty-five people working in Frankfurt, fifty of whom are German. In Silicon Valley in California, the epicentre of change in electronic commerce, 80% of staff members are American. However, it was originally Irish managers from the Dublin headquarters who went to the Valley and established our US headquarters, which is now an invaluable base of credibility in the region for Trintech.

I have always felt that it was important for Trintech to be a company that does not follow others but innovates to stay ahead of the competition. People remember who was first, and companies get a premium for being first. At Trintech, we have introduced an innovation ratio for measuring the contribution of new product development to overall revenues. Some 70% of our target revenues come from products developed in the previous three years. This shows just how important research and development is for our company and to that end, we spend a massive 29% of sales revenues on research and development. We have some 150 research and development staff in four centres – in Dublin and Frankfurt in Europe, and in San Mateo and Princeton, New Jersey, in the United States.

The company's early entry into the Internet payments software market has contributed to its series of industry firsts in electronic commerce. Trintech was the first company in the world to go live with a secure electronic payment transaction using a Visa card over the Internet. It was the world's first secure Internet purchase and was carried out by the president of Visa Argentina, who bought a bottle of wine from an Argentinean wine merchant over the Internet using Trintech software. The software allows credit card holders to shop on the Internet with the same confidence as in the physical world. Trintech was also in the first group of vendors that received the SET trademark from Visa International.

One of Trintech's core competencies is multi-currency transactions. Embracing new currencies is nothing new for Trintech because of our activity in Europe. Trintech completed the world's first euro transaction in Frankfurt, Germany, at the stroke of midnight on 1 January 1999. These industry firsts give Trintech significant 'mind share' in the market, which, in time, is turned into market share.

Strategic partners

From the beginning, I wanted to make sure that Trintech set about getting the right leaders and partners. We wanted to align ourselves with the captains of industry. People are judged on the basis of whom they associate with. Investors judge companies in the same way. If they see smart leaders and smart partners in a company, they will invest smart money. If investors see the Visa International corporation putting money into a payment company like Trintech, they conclude that Visa knows a thing or two about payments and their estimation of Trintech rises. That is how we maintain a respectable profile.

Trintech has developed strategic partnerships in the payment, data security, e-commerce and telephony industries, linking with such prolific and successful companies as Netscape, Microsoft, Compaq, Unisys, SAP, Motorola, Phone.com and Mastercard, as well as Visa International.

These relationships give us an invaluable credibility with our customers. We maintain contact with worldwide customers through both direct and indirect sales channels. Direct sales offices in Dublin, Frankfurt, San Mateo and Miami account for some 95% of revenue, but indirect sales, by way of e-commerce, will become a larger source of revenue in the future. To simplify sales and marketing operations, we have divided the world into three regions, namely Asia–Pacific; the Americas; and Europe, the Middle East and Africa. The Europe, Middle East and Africa region has traditionally provided most of our sales, with Germany being our largest customer. However, the Americas are fast becoming an area of growth for Trintech, with new direct-sales initiatives.

Capital and flotation

In 1998, with new product launches growing apace, Trintech looked to the future needs that would ensure continued growth. We already had an annual turnover of some $25 million, but roughly 45% of our revenues came from Germany, and it was important that we started focussing more on the US market. We needed greater visibility and credibility to begin an aggressive expansion plan in the US. To achieve this, we needed capital. There are various ways to raise capital. One option we considered at the time was to float the company on international stock markets. This would attract new shareholder capital. On the one hand, the capital acquired from going public would give us freedom to operate. On the other hand, we would be beholden to shareholders and open to the ravages of the stock market, and we would lose the privacy of accounts that is normal for a private company. In August 1998, we decided to postpone a public flotation and instead raised $20 million in private investment. We exchanged 16% of the company for the capital from a consortium of US investment banks and information technology companies. This valued the company at around $115 million. At the time, this was the largest single investment in an Irish software company.

Our biggest competitor, Verifone, had been bought by Hewlett–Packard for $1.15 billion in 1997. Verifone was generating annual revenues of $472 million at the time of its takeover. Clearly, we still had a lot of growth to achieve if we were to become the number one payment software company.

We sought more ways to achieve our investment plans in new markets and in 1999 looked seriously again at the right timing for a stock market flotation. In one year, we had doubled our workforce to 250 people, divided between our main US office in Silicon Valley, where John was based, and our new 25,000-square-foot facility in Leopardstown in Dublin. We decided that it would make good sense to float on two international stock markets – the German Neuer Markt and the New York-based Nasdaq Stock Market. Nasdaq alone might well have been sufficient, but we had a lot of custom in Germany and had achieved strong credibility there. We chose Europe also because investors here tend to be more long term in their decisions, and this would offset the greater volatility of Nasdaq investors, who tend to be more momentum-driven. We decided to float 23% of the company on both markets in September 1999. The 48% stake that John and I retained in Trintech would then be diluted to 36%, and institutional investors would dilute theirs from 49% to 38%. In advance of the flotation, we launched our prospectus and began a roadshow covering more than fifty cities worldwide to increase potential buyer interest. On 27 September 1999, Trintech shares were offered at $11.55 and €11 in a dual stock market listing. This was the first time ever that an Irish company had listed in Germany or indeed had dual-listed on the Nasdaq in New York and the Neuer Markt in Frankfurt. The sale of shares brought in $60 million, net of expenses, valuing the company at over $250 million. We now had the capital, and we needed to execute our plans.

The story of Trintech in the following months is fascinating. Within two months, the shares had soared, increasing by more than 130% in value. By early February 2000, investor confidence had boosted share value to more than $50. Then we announced a lucrative deal with Motorola at the GSM World Congress in Cannes. Trintech would combine its virtual credit card technology with Motorola's wireless devices to enable credit card payments by way of mobile phones. In the space of just one day after the announcement, Trintech shares rose by 20% on the Neuer Markt and 30% on the Nasdaq to trade at a high of over $76, seven times the flotation price. The growth of confidence in Trintech was exceptional. This confidence has been justified by a huge annual growth in revenues of almost 60% to some $49 million in 2000. Our decision to increase our spending on sales and marketing by more than 80% has borne fruit. At this rate, we are comfortable with the consensus on the street that we will report a profit in 2002. Flotation of the company was always in our sights as a business strategy. People might be swift to think that an initial public offering (IPO) is a means to an end, the end being to make the owners a lot of money. The IPO is not an exit. It is not an endgame but rather a whole new beginning. In fact, on the day of our IPO, the president of Nasdaq said to us: 'Today is the first day of the rest of your public life.'

New growth, responsibility and control

Trintech was capitalized at $1.2 billion, making us one of the top ten companies in Ireland. That is a great achievement, but I only ever look forward and never backwards. The achievement provides Trintech with a new currency, which allows us to acquire other companies and become the number one company in secure payments. By mid-2000, we were the largest payment technology company in the world. We have reached the pinnacle in our own sector. All that that says to me is that it is time to broaden and expand globally beyond that sector. I want to enter markets and countries where we are not as strong and areas where we are not as prominent. We have grown so much organically, on our own steam. Now it is time to use the currency of tradable shares to grow through acquisitions. In the four months to the beginning of 2001, we made a series of significant acquisitions that broadened our product suite, expanded our customer base and enabled our business to grow in other geographic regions of the world. In deals amounting to $112 million, we acquired a British firm, Checkline, a South American firm, Sursoft, a US-based competitor, Globeset, and an Irish company, Exceptis Technologies. Exceptis Technologies is itself a shining example of Irish enterprise. The company, originally called Peregrine Systems, was set up in 1992 by Bill O'Connor and Brian Caulfield and develops technology for fraud management and risk control of credit cards. It employs 60 people to service a highly respectable worldwide customer base of more than 50 financial institutions. The addition of these 60 employees has brought the Trintech workforce to more than 650.

There is certainly a responsibility in managing an entity of more than 650 people, but it neither discourages nor scares me. I do not worry about what I control, because I have confidence in my own actions and those of my management team. It is the factors outside my control that give cause for concern. To have achieved seven times our share offer price within a year of flotation is great. However, the volatility of the market is beyond my ability to influence. When the bull market changes to a bear market, halving the valuation of all technology stocks, people who own Trintech stock do not blame a faceless Wall Street. They point the finger at the face of Trintech – Cyril McGuire. That is beyond my control.

As a public company, we have to deal with added pressures in a volatile market. One of the reasons a public company must compile four reports a year rather than one is that the whole world can change in three months, and there is a need to track a company's performance against fixed milestones. Despite the market volatility affecting high-technology stocks, Trintech continues to grow. We have no debt and a bank balance of more than $100 million. We are here for the long term.

Ireland's Silicon Valley

The atmosphere has changed dramatically in Ireland in the last fifteen years. Going into business used to be a leap of faith in a culture of risk adversity. In recent years, a spirit of enterprise and risk-taking has been unleashed. Failure once meant a lifetime black mark. Now the most successful entrepreneur is one who has learnt from his or her mistakes. The current environment helps entrepreneurs to thrive in Ireland. People are benefitting from the influence of foreign high-tech companies. They are taking knowledge and skills from the multinationals and applying them in their own new enterprises. The government-backed industrial development bodies, Forfás, IDA Ireland and Enterprise Ireland (formerly Forbairt), dedicate great effort to supporting these enterprises. Trintech benefitted greatly from the support of Forbairt in the early years. The prosperity of the economy in the last ten years has resulted in a lot of surplus capital being made available for enterprise initiatives. Raising £250,000 ten years ago was a windfall investment. Now £250,000 is considered to be buttons, not even worth a press release. Unless £10 million is raised, people do not bat an eyelid in Ireland today.

There are also now strong precedents for Irish domestic and international successes. IONA, Trintech and Baltimore have hit the world stage on the Nasdaq. Every day the newspapers carry the story of yet another Irish multimillionaire. Ireland is now the high-tech hub of Europe and a terrific platform for enterprise.

All of these forces combine to generate the perfect environment, the perfect macro-economy in which to launch an enterprise. In the same way that a ship stays docked if a storm is brewing or the conditions are rough, you can only raise the sails of enterprise in the right environment.

Ireland has the atmosphere of Silicon Valley. When I go to the Valley, I get my batteries recharged. Anything is possible there. In the Valley, the glass is never half empty. Ireland has assumed that same positive attitude, that vibrancy. We still face coming to work drenched in the depth of winter, but that does not dampen the new spark of creativity.

The new environment and atmosphere has produced a new wave of entrepreneurs, a new breed of energetic young Irish people not willing to look at the past but facing the future with enthusiasm. They have the ability to attract capital. They have the government support systems. They have the precedents to beat, and they are very charged and ready to succeed.

Many people are anxious to throw their idea into a business plan and demand success in six months. Building a company takes time. A successful company has an inherent fabric – an inner being – that sustains it and must be slowly nurtured. Business plans for new enterprise ventures cross my desk regularly. As an investor in a number of start-up companies, I would look critically at a business plan for several important things. I call them the three P's to prosperity.

Firstly, I would look at the company's Product potential in its respective market. The market size must be of global proportion and growing rather than declining. A product targeting domestic market share only does not entice me. Furthermore, a product that faces multiple competitors, even in a global market, does not engage a high interest.

Secondly, I look to see what Partnerships the start-up has established. Who are the company shareholders that bring a little grey-haired credibility? Can I call a credible customer or supplier that will tell me the company's product is a killer idea? Who else has kicked the tyres of this venture and invested both time and money? For instance, Trintech secured the ex-CEO of Visa International as a board member and shareholder – a man with experience of working with every significant bank in the world and a reputation that preceded him in the industry.

Thirdly, and most importantly, I assess the People that make up the management team of this start-up company. A balanced management team with a good track record is unquestionably the number one criterion I look for. The balance must reside in the combination of skills the team shares. Typically, an entrepreneur will be either technically oriented or commercially oriented – it is rare to find both attributes in one individual. Therefore, the team must ideally share disciplines in technology expertise, finance, marketing and sales. John and I were fortunate to have a good balance of technological, financial and marketing skills. The track record of the management team could be in the fields of academia, industry or private business, as long as they have demonstrated a thirst to succeed, have learnt from any failures and have the ability to hold out until they win. A chequered career is not a bad thing. Serial entrepreneurs are by definition those who have tried several ventures and failed but who persist and eventually succeed. I myself have what I fondly refer to as a 'good diversified portfolio' of experience, running nightclubs and a Christmas tree company during my years at university.

Ultimately, a business plan must jump out at me. There has to be some element that makes it rise above the background noise and differentiates it from a hundred other business plans. As with any venture capital manager, I do not have the time to delve very deeply into a business plan, so there must be some aspect that is immediately and captivatingly compelling.

A new start-up venture can often benefit if it takes advantage of an incubator-style environment. Enterprise Ireland offers incubator support that provides seed funding and the facility to network with other similar companies. It is very lonely and daunting at the launch of a start-up, especially if one tries to be a solo promoter. Entrepreneurs by their nature are often confident and headstrong, but there is no shame in accepting help. We were happy with the worthwhile help that Forbairt provided to Trintech at its inception, and they were happy to receive just rewards through the growth in value of the Trintech shares they held. The industrial promotion agencies are rightly benefitting from equity participation in fledgling companies and can act with a self-sufficiency that reduces their demand on government resources.

The consequences of success

It is wonderful to witness the exceptional growth of enterprise, but in some ways we are the victims of our own success. The mentality of making a fast buck is creeping in. People want overnight success at any expense. Sometimes I wonder if there is more money than brains in town. Because wealth has come so quickly to so many, there is an unfortunate inclination to flippancy.

Enterprise activity is so vibrant that Ireland is running out of core skill sets. I now recruit most of my people outside the country, as it is difficult to get the highly skilled engineers that we need. We need to recruit another 250 people in the next 18 months to fill the latest addition to our facility in Leopardstown. One of the advantages of having a global footprint is that we also have access to the world's skill pool. A recent poll of our Dublin staff shows the number of nationalities to be fourteen – a reflection of the mature and diverse Ireland with which we are very comfortable in our workforce. The skills shortages are driving wages higher and contributing to price inflation. This in turn fuels the rise in prices in the property market, which completes a vicious circle of higher wage demands. This has the potential of making Ireland a less competitive environment from an industry perspective.

The inflation and the skills shortages are clear evidence of overstretching in the economy. I only hope for a soft landing when the economy descends. Despite economic cycles, I think the spirit of enterprise is here for good. We are a young population that is unquestionably more confident and unquestionably better off. The up-and-down cycles of the future can only make us more resilient.

At the end of the day

I personally approach the concept of newly found wealth with the adage 'health above wealth' in mind. I try to achieve a good balance between social, sporting and business pursuits. Obviously, I spend a lot of time in business because I enjoy it, but I get rid of any frustration on the sports field, playing football or golf. I keep a very active social life because I love personal interaction. Trintech is not just a technology company, it is a people company, and the personal touch is important to me. There is a lot of growth to manage in Trintech. If we can hold our heads, add good people and continue on our present track, we will be a very successful high-tech company. That said, if I am healthy and enjoying life in ten years, I will be a happy man.

MARY MANGAN

Chief operating officer, ireland.com;
Former managing director, buyandsell.net;
Former managing director, PostGEM/Ireland On-Line

Mary Mangan exudes an energy that is immediately engaging. She speaks earnestly, with a pristine, clear-thinking control, and at the same time conveys an infectious sense of enthusiasm. One might think that a woman who has worked seriously in a remarkable seven different major companies would be world-weary and willing to settle for a quiet life. Instead, she confides that she is inherently restless and always looking for challenge and change. She thrives in a changing environment and since this interview has turned her hand to applying her considerable experience in operations management to the transient Internet world as chief operations officer of ireland.com.

Her natural warmth is strongest when she talks of her family, her friends and her love of Ireland. In fact, her desire to stay relatively close to her roots in the west of Ireland has resulted in her turning down international managerial roles in major multinationals. Indeed, in the end, the things she values most are simple and beyond the business world. Success is a glass of wine and good food with her husband and daughter at the end of the week.

However, her personal warmth in no way impedes her capacity to make hard-headed business decisions. A catchphrase *of hers is, 'There were casualties along the way!' Her one regret is not making the leap from the corporate world to full enterprise autonomy ten years earlier. However, hearing her story, it seems that for this relatively young enterprise leader, none of her work has been wasted time.*

Early catalysts

I come from an enterprising background. I was immersed in an enterprise culture from a young age, as my family was involved in managing typical country enterprises – pubs, shops and undertaking. My father was a man with a rudimentary education, but he built a very successful set of businesses during the latter half of the 1950s and 1960s. Somebody said to me in jest recently, 'Mary, you've never been a worker, you've always been a boss', but I replied, 'I used to be a worker years ago at home serving tables.' When I was young, I started as a junior helper at entertainment functions, went on to become head waitress and progressed until I willingly took on the responsibility of organizing large weddings. There were never any hang-ups about workplace equality in my family, as my mother played a key role in sustaining the businesses through her financial management and administration skills. Our family businesses succeeded as a result of the shared dedication of each member. Each individual contributed to the whole. You can break one stick but not a bunch tied together. So teamwork and the ability to contribute were things that I learnt early on. A lot of enterprising people have some element in their background that has acted as an ultimate catalyst. I learnt a lot growing up as the daughter of an enterprising business family.

My parents had the idea that I should not go into business

but should rather choose a safe career. They probably wanted to ensure that I did not have to endure the emotional hardship and long and hard work hours that they associated with business through their own experience. They wanted an easier lifestyle for me. Originally, I set out to study pharmacy but changed my mind to study more interesting industrial chemistry at University College Dublin. I loved the challenge in my studies, particularly that in mathematics.

Growing in five major companies

When I graduated, I joined Cement Roadstone and worked in their research and development facility. I soon found that I did not like the everyday 'grunge' of research and gravitated towards work that involved doing a lot of promoting and selling of the products we developed. I was frustrated by the painstaking day-to-day work of pure research, especially when our bright ideas did not work out. I really wanted to become a front person and get more involved in taking products to the marketplace.

An opportunity to realize this desire arose in 1983 when IBM undertook a major recruitment drive to build their capacity as an industry solutions provider. My husband, Philip, worked for IBM at the time, so I felt that I already knew the culture at IBM with a familiar warmth. I had very little computing knowledge and thought it would be worthwhile to add this to my skills in sales and marketing. There was an enormous global hype about information technology at the time, so I thought, 'What the heck', and joined IBM.

In terms of what has happened since in my career, that decision has proved to be the most important I have made. It was important because it was my first move into information technology. IBM also invested very significantly in their staff, and I received excellent training and mentoring throughout my four years there. I was fortunate to work for an enlightened manager, who allowed me to chase my ideas. I was a bolshy young woman, and since IBM did not have many of those at the time, they were very tolerant of me.

If there is one thing I learnt from IBM, it is that 'people buy from people'. The ability to build strong working relationships with customers defines success or failure. That relationship need not necessarily be love and kisses all the time, but it should be one that is built on trust, honesty and integrity. Such a relationship will be mutually beneficial. I believe that customer relationships are fostered by a strong human element of regular contact. Fostering customer relations is one job that is simply not facilitated by 'virtual working'. I currently live in Ballymore Eustace and have a fully functional virtual office at home. I occasionally spend days working from home, but I much prefer to be in town, where I can bump into people and 'be there' for lunch in five minutes. Being instantly available is the way I like doing business.

By 1987 I was at the stage where I wanted to move into a management role. I felt I needed more expertise in people management, an area in which I felt I was inadequate. I still criticize myself today for not being the best people manager. There were no such opportunities in IBM, and Hewlett–Packard came knocking on the door looking for someone to be the country sales manager. I immediately thought to myself, 'This is the opportunity I have been waiting for.' At the same time I asked myself, 'Am I going to be able to do this?' I found that it was an even bigger job than I had thought.

Hewlett–Packard was not in particularly good shape when I joined. They had some super people but had not developed a product line for the Irish marketplace. They had a very expensive personal computer range and a technically excellent but expensive peripheral product range. I did two things. Firstly, I set about working with the existing team to build a company sales strategy and recruited the additional people we needed to construct a great team to execute that strategy. Secondly, I led the charge into new markets.

We built Hewlett–Packard's 'systems integration' capability such that we could sell and deliver both software and hardware solutions to Irish companies. These solutions were based around existing Hewlett–Packard products and services, but we also bundled products and services from other suppliers to offer an end-to-end solution to our customers. On the back of this capability, we closed a significant number of coveted systems integration contracts, including systems for the Department of Defence, Beaumont Hospital, the Department of Education and the Naval Service. We also launched new products into the Irish marketplace, for example the Vectra personal computer and printer product ranges. We set up a completely new dealer distribution network, and this helped us to win many large public- and private-sector contracts. The extended team grew the business substantially over the next four years. It was a great break to get the opportunity to work in a growing, evolving company with a youthful and dynamic atmosphere.

In 1990, the business was growing at a rapid pace, and we were struggling to use the resources of the corporation efficiently in the Irish market. We looked at how we could leverage the capabilities of Hewlett–Packard in the United Kingdom. I suggested that we strip out the top Irish management layer and plug Ireland into the UK organization to enable access to those skills and resources and at the same time reduce local costs. Effectively, I was doing myself out of a job. I felt, indeed, that I had done the job for which I had been enlisted. Hewlett–Packard offered me a management position in London. My husband and I went on a reconnaissance weekend to London, looked at the bedlam, the traffic and the lifestyle and decided to forget it in favour of staying in Ireland. It was vitally important for both of us to focus on maintaining a fulfilling and stable family life – a wish that has always remained in our hearts. I had just had my daughter, Rebecca, and the idea of living in London with its commuting chaos and isolation from our extended family network was far from appealing. Given that decision, I find it ironic today that I spend the same amount of time commuting from Kildare to my Dublin office as many of my friends do commuting from Dublin to London.

At the time, ICL in Ireland was undergoing a huge transformation in response to being thrashed in its own market by Hewlett–Packard and IBM. ICL management understood that the company had to change fundamentally in order to overcome the competition. They wanted somebody who could come into their top management team and act as a catalyst for that change. I decided I could fill this role and joined them as a marketing manager. I worked in particular with the managing director to effect a culture of change and a spirit of buying into our vision of reinventing the company. We designed a radical five-year plan for the business that would bring in fresh blood and make substantial changes to the organization and the product structure – and yes, there were casualties along the way. Ultimately, we also paved the way for a new managing director.

Within two years, I was satisfied that the original job was done, and I was asked to set up a new ICL personal computer business. I hated it. The dealer business was at that time very immature in Ireland. I was very uncomfortable with the individuals involved and struggled with their business ethics.

Nevertheless, I headed up the personal computer division in Ireland for one year and restructured the business model such that the distribution and management of the dealer network was outsourced. At the end of the year I asked to be changed to another role, and I was asked to set up a government business unit for ICL in Dublin. Within six months, we had secured a multimillion-pound government contract. This started the business, and we went on to have an outstanding three years – this was work I knew I was good at.

As ICL evolved, we drew on the resources of other large companies, one of which happened to be AT&T. They wanted somebody to manage several Irish projects and explore new business opportunities in the Internet field. I knew very little about the Internet and thought once again that it would be a great opportunity to work with an exciting new medium while staying in Ireland. I took the job and spent some time in the United Kingdom watching and learning how AT&T made strategic investments in Internet companies by investing their technology in return for equity or revenue share. I had the good fortune to work on innovative Internet projects involving Barclays Bank and pop artist George Michael's Aegean Project. George Michael had found a new vent for his creativity and wanted to set up his own online record label. I was very impressed by this major star, who showed great enterprise in recognizing the potential of online business at such an early stage in the development of the Internet.

Managing director at last

I was beginning to earn a reputation as someone with good knowledge of Internet businesses when I was approached to become managing director of PostGEM/Ireland On-Line (IOL).

Mary Mangan

Denis O'Brien

Photograph courtesy of Frank Fennell

Pádraig Ó Céidigh

Pat and Annette Shanahan

Brody Sweeney

Louis Walsh

Photograph courtesy of Matt Kavanagh

Carole Ward

I was thrilled with the opportunity, not only because of the responsibility I would hold but also because I felt that I was spending too much of my life in hotels in the United Kingdom. I had put on two stone in two years and was not seeing enough of my family. I thought, 'To hell with this', and came back to Ireland.

PostGEM was a pure data company, providing data solutions and business-to-business services for large corporate customers. IOL was an Internet access provider for consumer and small-business customers. I will never forget my first day. There was much to improve. Effectively, I had two companies with two sets of management teams and a huge amount of unnecessary overhead. I could have looked at it as a difficult situation but instead saw it as a marvellous opportunity. As I met with the staff and customers of both businesses, I quickly realized that I had an outstanding pool of talented people who were dedicated to developing the business and driving it forward. They were crying out for the leadership and direction that would bring about the change needed in the businesses.

I brought a lot of focus to PostGEM/IOL. I built a new combined management team, and while there were casualties along the way, we introduced some fantastic new people. Together we turned a company culture of extreme confusion into one of clear definition, in which people understood clearly their roles and responsibilities.

We defined the businesses better and built sets of products with solid marketing strategies that would ensure their success. We restructured the organization of human resources in a way that empowered people to take whatever initiatives they felt were required to meet customers' needs. In this way, we adopted a real customer-centred culture in the businesses.

In my own role, I tried to adopt an operating style of being very firm, very fair and, above all, consistent. In a company that had been allowed to get somewhat out of control, I found that I was perhaps even something of a dictator at times. I was pushy and drove my management team hard. During the process of transformation for improvement, we gave people what we thought was a lot of support and an adequate period of time to make the required change, but if they were not willing to make the changes in that period of time, they were effectively opting out. We enlisted the help of an external consulting company to help us to bring the improvements to fruition in the company, and this proved to be very worthwhile and successful. It was a difficult and stressful process, and I probably did not make a lot of friends along the way. However, I believe I did gain the respect of the majority of the staff, and we did ultimately achieve the results we wanted.

PostGEM improved dramatically. We improved its results significantly. We maintained IOL's position as the leading Internet service provider (ISP) until the arrival of the BT/ESB joint venture, Ocean, which was the first 'free' ISP service in Ireland. By then, we had established PostGEM/IOL as a lucrative takeover target and eventually sold the company to Denis O'Brien's Esat for £115 million in September 1999.

Bricks to clicks

After the sale, I took a week off for my brother's wedding in Cork. I used the time to reflect on my options. I had the offer of a position in Esat, running a data business with £140 million annual turnover, but that would have entailed handing over the autonomy I so much enjoyed.

As it happened, the offer to create and run buyandsell.net emerged. I loved the bricks-to-clicks concept of transforming a traditional and successful paper into an e-business entity. The

Buy and Sell paper had established a very successful business as the market-leading paper for free classified ads. With 92% brand recognition among adults and a readership of 500,000, there was little sense of urgency in the move to change a successful business model. However, there was a growing awareness that the forces of the new economy were moulding a new environment around us. We had the choice to see this as either a threat or an opportunity. We decided to embrace the opportunity and not only enhance the existing business but offer something greater to customers with a new online service, which we would launch as buyandsell.net. Buyandsell.net would have a new and inclusive partnership philosophy that brought shareholders, suppliers, staff and customers closer together. Each of the shareholders would have a coherent belief in the vision of the business, as well as having the fleetness of foot required to adapt to the changing demands of an online environment. The *Buy and Sell* paper, with its strong brand recognition and distribution networks, became the cornerstone of the new partnership. Nevada Tele.com added their technical expertise to the partnership and also provided the telecommunications and Internet infrastructure to make buyandsell.net an online reality. Finally, a venture capital partner brought the funds, business contacts, expertise and market credibility needed to achieve a successful launch in November 1999. Importantly, our customers also play an integral role in the partnership, through the provision of 5% of the company to customers. It is a win–win strategy that enables us to return favour and goodwill to the people who ultimately sustain the business, while ensuring growth in customer loyalty.

The energy, funds and time invested in creating buyandsell.net have been justified by the results. Since its launch, the site has consistently been one of the top ten most popular Irish websites. The revenues have grown month on month such that the site began running at a profit sooner than targeted. Most importantly, the increase in visibility of Buy and Sell has contributed to the growth of the paper arm. Circulation has increased by 10%, advertising revenues have grown, and profits have soared by 27%. The migration from bricks to clicks has been clearly worth it. As for future growth and innovation, watch this e-space!

The new economy

From my own perspective, creating an online enterprise has been a truly enjoyable and hugely educational experience. My understanding of electronic commerce in the new economy has grown significantly. The new economy can be described in terms of the manner in which companies have adopted three new important ways of working: shifting the emphasis from a company's tangible assets to its intangible assets; taking full advantage of new information-technology tools; and employing a workforce that is mobile and flexible. The new economy is a global phenomenon, and yet Irish companies have shown a particular openness to these new ways of working and an ability to embrace them successfully.

It makes no sense to waste money holding tangible inventory in huge warehouses when you can outsource this to professional and specialist companies. In Ireland, for instance, Green Isle Foods achieved a massive cost reduction and doubled the turnover of their Goodfellas Pizza division within five years as a result of new supplier relationships and reduced stockholding. The intangible assets that assume great importance in the new economy include product design and innovation, brand, market insight, management and staff know-how, and strong customer relationships. Businesses such as buyandsell.net can be built on the back of these intangible assets. Exploitation of information technology makes possible new ways of conducting business and structuring a company. Customers are empowered with information about the variety of sellers and products in the marketplace and are far more selective. From the sellers' perspective, many more customers can be accessed in new markets. The ability of companies to work in real time with information about events as they unfold drives the need to become very agile and adaptable. The need for increased agility in turn drives the need for a far more flexible workforce. Flexible work hours, virtual team working, and the mobility to travel to meet customers in new markets are key company work practices in the new economy. In return for this flexibility, new incentives, from staff ownership of the company to casual dress codes, have become the norm. The power of the new economy is underlined by the fact that these three new ways of working complement each other. For example, less tangible and fixed assets give staff a freedom of mobility, while information technology permits constant communication in a mobile and virtual organization.

There is no alternative

A fundamental of the new economy is that business leadership today is no guarantee of success tomorrow. Certainly in any service industry, and probably in most manufacturing industries, change is not optional. One of the barriers to change is that firms are frightened that they will cannibalize their existing customers. The reality is that if they do not cannibalize their customers, someone else will. Competition will emerge from two sources: traditional competitors who may be moving part of their business online; and, probably more threateningly, new players who come to the market without the baggage of management culture and worries about upsetting traditional ways of working. In Ireland, a new breed of young, enterprising, e-commerce contenders are gaining footholds in traditional business markets. They do not accept the assumptions or constraints of traditional businesses. They work by an entirely new set of rules. They have mastered the rapidly converging communications, computing and content technologies. Furthermore, they understand the need to create new business models to gain speed-to-market advantages. One of the major benefits of the new economy is that it has slashed time to market. In 'Internet time', new businesses can be launched in dramatically short timescales. Traditional bricks-and-mortar businesses must realize that the world does not seem to be moving faster – it is moving faster.

If a company decides to make the leap from bricks to clicks, the choice of partnerships that will facilitate the change is crucial. Traditionally, bricks-and-mortar companies operated with a 'Do It Yourself' model. Clicks organizations are finding it more effective and less expensive to collaborate in partnerships. Alliances must be chosen far more selectively than in the past, as the Web economy is unforgiving. A recent survey by Zona Research of California found that 61% of Internet alliances are viewed as disappointments or failures. Only 39% have met or exceeded expectations. Traditionally, companies may have had the luxury of changing alliances and partners that do not work out. However, the Internet, because of the impact of 'Internet time' and the importance of customer relationships, is far less forgiving. The operations of a new-economy company are equally important. In the same survey, ten leading US retail websites showed that 39% of all attempts to buy products on the site failed, while 56% of all search requests failed. How long would a traditional business last if 56% of customers could not find what they wanted and nearly 40% failed to purchase what they had found? The research also estimated that slow download time alone put some $4.3 billion in e-commerce sales at risk each year. Many customers who fail to complete a search or a purchase never come back. On the Internet, the competition is just a click away. It is no good getting the strategy right if the nuts and bolts do not work. The new economy rewards those who innovate. Creative thinking, of which there is no shortage in Ireland, is needed to take full advantage of the Internet in the promotion of Irish companies and their services and products. The Internet is a relatively new phenomenon. It is certain that not all the good ideas have been exploited.

Looking back on it, my decision to start buyandsell.net provided a greenfield opportunity not to be missed in an utterly fantastic enterprise climate in Ireland. A huge amount of enterprise excitement was being fuelled by groundbreaking deals such as the PostGEM/IOL sale. Companies such as Trintech and IONA led the charge of Irish success stories. Serious international attention was being turned to emerging Irish enterprises.

Only the bolshy survive

In the last ten years, Irish people have pulled themselves up by their bootstraps. We have developed the guts and the gumption not to fear failure and to realize that we are as good as anyone else. The most exciting aspect of our strengthening economy is the success of indigenous companies. These companies are contributing to the economy and the quality of life by their success on a local and international scale.

Government industrial development bodies are rightly focussing on encouraging indigenous enterprise. We have perhaps been too dependent on foreign multinationals, although they have played an important role in furthering our progress. We must now foster more enterprise and more research and development activity in this country.

An important development that must be encouraged is the involvement of women in enterprise. I think there are two reasons why we do not see more female chief executives in Ireland. The first is culture. A traditional attitude that female roles should be confined to homemaking, nursing and teaching was pervasive in girls' education and upbringing until the 1980s. This is now changing and rightly so. Secondly, glass ceilings still exist for women in business. Business structures and institutions have been moulded in a way that was sensible and suitable for the men who created them. Women have to have a hard neck to crack the old-boy networks, the black-tie dinners and the golf outings. The bolshy will survive.

Changing the bias will be an evolutionary rather than a revolutionary process. I always ask prospective employees how they feel about working for a woman. It is different from working for a man, and unless the difference is appreciated, they will struggle. In my company environment, the atmosphere is far more relaxed than in a traditional male-dominated company. I delegate avidly and give people the space to operate with freedom. I do not interfere unless there is a problem and need not be involved in every decision – it is more democratic.

Sometimes I wonder if I would like to see my daughter, Rebecca, launch herself into the business environment. It makes me reflect on my own experience. As a woman, I have had to work twice as hard. I have a tremendous sense of achievement, but it was dog hard to realize. I would probably tell her that there are easier ways to make a living. However, a recent horse-riding episode gave me a hint of her character. She jumps a course of 1.5-foot fences with her peers. I had just jumped a 3.5-foot course and heard Rebecca asking the horse-riding teacher if she could also jump the course. The teacher explained that even 2-foot fences would be too high for her. Rebecca insisted on trying 3 feet and proceeded to jump the course clear. She had never jumped that before, but a competitive instinct made her stretch herself. I got a kick from seeing that and guessed that she has the competitive drive. I just hope life will be easier for her.

Success is . . .

I get most personal fulfilment from Philip and Rebecca. I am hugely committed to enjoying them. Success to me is the three of us going out for dinner on a Friday night. At the end of the day, career success affords a nice standard of living. If that had been at the expense of my family, I would have failed.

Buyandsell.net will continue to grow in the years ahead. Success here means a sale or an initial public offering and personal reward for all the staff. I am getting involved in other businesses. I am the type of person who gets restless when my work is done. When things are on an even keel, I am already looking for the next challenge. I want to become involved in guiding a number of companies, while staying in Ireland. I love the life here – friends, family and culture. What I really love about being Irish is the way we look at things. Although we are serious about succeeding in our enterprises, we certainly know how to enjoy success when we achieve it.

DENIS O'BRIEN

Chairman, Communicorp;

Former chairman and CEO, Esat Telecom Group

*D*enis O'Brien invites me to sit at the round glass table in his *expansive office. The office is decorated with tasteful pop art. Abstract timepieces and sculptures fill a bookshelf, and, in all, fourteen framed* Time *magazine covers hang on the walls. Through the window and over the Grand Canal basin, the Dublin skyline is visible, punctuated by the cranes that are shaping the city.*

Denis O'Brien's enterprise ventures are characterized by their diversity. After studying history, politics and logic at University College Dublin and taking an MBA at Boston College, he spent several years working directly with Tony Ryan of Guinness Peat Aviation (GPA). He cut his teeth on a failed TV shopping channel, funding his investment by selling horse healthcare products for his father's company in the United States. He successfully led a consortium bid to obtain the 98FM radio licence and managed a station that became Dublin's popular choice. Successful again in securing a licence to operate a data and fax communication company called Éireann Satellite (Esat), he piloted the company through years of growth and costly expansion, taking full advantage of gradual liberalization of the telecommunications sector in Ireland. He challenged and overcame the entrenched state monopoly of Telecom Éireann (now Eircom) in the relatively short timeframe of his stewardship. In 1995 he guided an Esat-led consortium bid to win the second national mobile phone licence *and shaped Esat's explosive growth thereafter. He floated the Esat group at $13 a share in November 1997 and sold the company to British Telecom at $100 a share in January 2000. The consequent IR£250 million personal gain facilitated a wider field of vision. Advanced technology investments in Ireland have been accompanied by investments such as the Dutch telecom venture Versatel, European golf courses, Portuguese property and a Jamaican mobile network. However, Ireland has always featured in his most ambitious plans, as shown by his ePower venture for electricity generation and distribution and, more famously, in his bid for the fixed-line business of his old rival, Eircom.*

Contributing to Ireland's social and economic development has been an indirect consequence of his enterprise throughout his career. However, contributing directly to development through education has become a passion in recent years. He played an early role in attracting to Ireland the prestigious MIT Media Lab – a centre of intellectual and academic excellence that fuses the physical and virtual worlds. A donation of £3 million to the Michael Smurfit Business School at Carysfort has improved computing and intranet facilities in the school. Furthermore, he is chairman of the Organizing Committee of the Special Olympics, to be held in Ireland in 2003, and takes an active interest in Amnesty International.

Early learning

Way back when I began working as an assistant to Tony Ryan, chief executive of Guinness Peat Aviation, I learnt how big companies work. Big companies have tremendous wells of power, and to see how power can be given, controlled and taken back is very intriguing. Working in a big company environment means working on a big canvas where the opportunities to express oneself and to influence others are exciting. For instance, in 1975, not many people would have imagined that by 1992, GPA would have come close to realizing the grand vision of controlling the world's aircraft leasing market, having created a new business model that had changed the face of the aviation industry.

Having been introduced to the communications world by Fred O'Donovan, former RTÉ chairman, I undertook extensive research for GPA on direct broadcast satellite systems and was responsible for GPA's participation in a consortium that made a bid for the sole national licence to launch a direct broadcast satellite system. Little did I know at the time that such early learning in communications would be so valuable in starting Esat Telecom. I recall one weekend when I met some friends in Paris on a short break. I arrived an hour late at the meeting place of a friend's apartment, brandishing a large-sized scale model of the *Ariane* space rocket. My bemused friends thought I had found a new toy, but I insisted that communication satellites were the 'way of the future', a conviction that was blindly prophetic.

I also learnt three key elements to good people management at GPA. Firstly, be tough but fair. If you have an issue with someone, there's no point in annihilating them in front of peers. I think it's better to rule by performance than by fear. Secondly, hire the best people you can get your hands on. We have always tried to do just that. It might be expensive, but it pays off. Even so, I find that about a third of senior management don't work out, and you have to shoot them. Thirdly, but most importantly, give everyone an incentive to work hard. Everybody working to achieve a goal, from management to assistants, must share in the spoils. Ideally, a share option scheme should provide returns to employees that far outstrip salaries, and the people who have worked with us bear testament to that. Not every Irish company realizes the importance of incentives for employees, but GPA always had a good incentive culture.

Wealth culture

In principle, there are no downsides when people win large sums of money through such incentive schemes, but sudden wealth can indeed affect the way people think. Beyond the financial rewards for the Esat management team, some IR£250 million was divided among Esat staff members at the time of our takeover by British Telecom. Many went on holidays to Florida or built an extension at home and didn't take advantage of the fact that 'money makes money'. A windfall of £100,000 could be better invested to return £300,000 in five years. In one way, easy money tends to destroy an individual's thinking.

An easy-money culture can take hold of a city or a country and detract from the pursuit of other worthwhile values. People's values change if they are not used to handling money. It depends greatly on the individual. In my estimation, about 50% of people do not manage sudden wealth very well. A bad thing can be the loss of friends as people try to move into a different social stratum and forget about their roots. People forget that old friends are best.

It is good to have a balance between an unfettered economy and a socially progressive culture. I think Ireland can achieve this balance. Much of our management training and culture comes directly from North America through technology and multinational companies. However, we are Irish and Europeans and should set this US business ethic into the context of good social thinking.

Consortia, failure and success

While I promoted GPA's involvement in direct broadcast satellite systems, I also started to play an assisting role in my father's business, Plusvital, which manufactured and distributed food supplement and horse care products for thoroughbred horses. Every month I spent two weeks on the road in the United States, setting up wholesalers and dealers across twenty states. One night, as I watched television from a motel room in Lexington, Kentucky, I came across the television Home Shopping Network (HSN). I was immediately struck by the simplicity of the concept and the potential to apply it to a consumer audience in Europe. The next day, I jumped on a plane to Tampa, Florida, and walked into the HSN headquarters without even an appointment. I was given a tour of the facilities and met with the top executives to discuss the operations of the network. I offered to form a European partnership with them, but unfortunately they decided to maintain an insular, US focus on their home market. I left Tampa with what I thought was a 'killer' business idea.

Within a short space of time, I rallied a consortium of Irish investors and set up Éireann Satellite Television to launch a shopping channel in the United Kingdom. We formed a partnership with a large mail order company, Grattan plc, which had a large stock of attractive merchandise, and leased transmission time from Sky Television for broadcasting. The start-up of the channel went smoothly in terms of operations. However, from a financial point of view, the venture was in trouble from the outset. In our first month, we turned over £14,000 and lost £500,000. While daily sales eventually reached £170,000, we never managed to cover expenses, and eighteen months after the launch, we finally decided that we had failed and closed down the Shopping Channel. I was initially shattered by the weight of failure. However, in retrospect, this episode has been a major help to my understanding of volatility and the inherent risks of business. In subsequent years, I found that US venture capital managers and investment bankers were far more interested in funding my enterprise ventures when they heard that I had put a solid failure behind me in my portfolio of experiences.

The first major enterprise success that I achieved was with the radio station Classic Hits 98FM. I was aware that new radio licences would become available, and when they were advertised, I decided to put a consortium together to bid for the licence. I just picked up the phone and asked people I was comfortable with if they wanted to be involved. Only one person declined. We were conscious that many very successful radio stations already existed and were thriving, so we made sure that our bid would meet the requisite criteria in every way. To that end, we put together an eclectic group to show inclusiveness and represent every interest and walk of life. The consortium members included James Donnelly, chairman of Northern Ireland's Downtown Radio; Frank Murphy, general manager of the National Concert Hall; Labhras Ó Murchú, director-general of Comhaltas Ceoltóirí Éireann; Éamonn O'Doherty, a former Commissioner of An Garda Síochána; Liz Howard, a successful sportswoman and flight service manager in Aer Lingus; Liam Ó Murchú, the RTÉ presenter; Ciaran Fitzgerald, international and Lions rugby cap and captain of the winning Triple Crown Irish rugby team; Luke Mooney, a financial advisor; and my father and me.

I had only a 3% or 4% stake, as I had no money whatsoever – the Shopping Channel debacle had left me with little funds. The remainder of the funding, some £150,000, came from shareholders of the Shopping Channel, who viewed it as a follow-on investment. We hired KPMG to ensure a consistency of thought and to write the proposal. Unfortunately, we did not win a national licence. This was a blow, because winning or losing would define my standing as an entrepreneur. I reshaped the consortium, changing some of the backers, and went after a Dublin licence, this time successfully. It was a lot of fun – with diverse people around a table, you can never predict what will happen. The new station, 98FM, went on to become Dublin's most popular commercial radio station. We built on our success, and from 1992 we set up similar stations in Prague and Stockholm. The Prague station became hugely successful with the help of new and powerful marketing techniques. Czech people had never seen the 'thunder parade' of our brand-new and eye-catching four-wheel-drive convoys. The station suddenly became a model for all things modern and youthful.

Esat Telecom

Three-quarters of the 98FM board continued with me to form the Esat Telecom consortium. We had no predefined plan other than to compete with Telecom Éireann. We drafted an initial business plan, but when I look back on it now, I ask myself how we ever managed to put money on it. It was by no means plain sailing from the start. While I had a strong and credible board behind me, I needed to find solid and dependable executives to work with me. I met an old friend whom I had not seen in years, Mark Roden, at a wedding in Kilkea Castle, Co. Kildare. He told me how he had just completed a coveted MBA from the Institute of Management and Administration in Switzerland. I was impressed, but when I asked him if he considered himself a businessman, he was surprised. We chatted, and soon after, he decided to leave the safety of his new consulting job in London to join me in Esat Telecom.

Together we built a full executive team, and in late 1991 and early 1992, we applied to the government for licences to operate satellite communication services. We submitted two licences that fell completely on deaf ears and did not even receive an acknowledgement. It was clear from the beginning that the government of the day was intent on preserving the state monopoly of Telecom Éireann. A year after our first application, the government finally acknowledged a third application and eventually granted us a licence to transmit data and faxes but strictly no voice telephony. We were in business at last, but highly restricted. Furthermore, we were dependent on Telecom Éireann to lease their fixed lines to Esat for data and fax transmission, and the lethargy of their co-operation was killing us slowly.

For four years we struggled to build a corporate customer base, and we had attracted only ninety-three customers by the end of 1994. In that year we also secured $10 million funding from Advent International, a venture capital company. This funding was helpful, but it was fairly insignificant in comparison with our full financial needs. Key executives sacrificed their salaries for months on end. We had serious cash-flow difficulties in meeting the salary payments for our regular staff. One wintry Friday night, we sat up into the early hours working and revising the cash-flow figures. After long hours of checking and cross-checking, we realized that we could not pay our staff the following week. We were short £50,000 and facing closure if we could not find the money. Leslie Buckley, whom I had hired as a management consultant to help build up the organization, went home to speak to his wife about their personal savings. Leslie had known me for less than a year but decided to lend £50,000 of his savings to enable Esat to survive for another two weeks. It is people of his kind who have breathed life into the company to save it when help was most desperately needed.

Cash-flow problems continued to haunt us. A full five years were spent on the edge and hanging on. In fact, in October 1995, the management team sat together deciding whether to put Esat into examinership. I had just earned £2 million from an IFSC (Irish Financial Services Centre) property investment and wanted to use that to save Esat. The advice from my father and my solicitor, Owen O'Connell, was that I would be out of my mind to invest in it. Advent International was aware of our difficulties and offered to invest enough to keep the company solvent. The offer came with a high price. Advent insisted that I step down as chief executive officer and relinquish the reins of the company. They proposed increasing Advent's shareholding to 66% from 33%. I would have had to dilute to 33%. At this time we had applied for the second national GSM licence, and I decided to await the outcome of our bid before deciding.

Upwardly mobile

The GSM bid faced major international competition of the highest quality. AT&T and Motorola were among the competing consortia that we faced, and their lobbying influence on the Irish government was significant. We had agreed a partnership to form a new GSM company, Esat Digifone, with Dermot Desmond's investment company, International Investment and Underwriting, and with the Norwegian state telephone company, Telenor. We delivered our completed application to the Department of Communications in Kildare Street with some flair. I suggested that we create a

Viking invasion by way of a street event that would wind its way through the city and arrive at the Department's offices. We hired a 40-foot juggernaut and transformed it into a Viking ship, with 24 staff dressed as Vikings and 12 glass boxes that contained our bid. The startled porter in the foyer of the Department's office building could not believe it when he was greeted by the *Eurovision* winner playing 'Nocturne' on her fiddle. The whole Department was hanging out the windows.

Twenty-four hours before the bid announcement, a fax arrived from Advent International. It stated that Advent had little faith in the potential for success of our GSM licence application; highlighted the latest financial difficulties that we faced; and requested that I step down from my position. I shredded it and went for a sandwich lunch with close colleagues Paul Connolly and Leslie Buckley. I remember confiding to them how close we were to folding the company. I had been invited to address Trinity College students on the subject of launching and running a business and felt myself to be an inappropriate lecturer, given the volatility of my business and my position. Two days later Minister Michael Lowry announced that we had won the bid. I was ecstatic. Esat's luck had suddenly turned, and everybody wanted to be our friend. Within months we closed a $27 million investment deal with a consortium of investors, paid off our creditors and secured a $112 million loan facility from AIB and ABN Amro banks.

We then faced the challenge of building a full national GSM network in a matter of months. In hopeful anticipation of winning the bid, we acquired purchasing options over more than 100 sites for the erection of network masts. However, planning permission delays averaged some ten months, whereas we were racing to achieve a six-month deadline agreed with the Department of Communications. Our frustrations were at last alleviated when we struck a deal, spearheaded by Conor Lenihan and affectionately referred to at the time by my management team as 'Project Blue', with the Garda Síochána. They allowed us to make use of their 700 existing masts in return for a new communications network. This was a very useful solution, as the Garda masts had already acquired planning approval and were strategically placed in the heart of every town and village in the country.

Esat thrived in the competitive environment of an increasingly deregulated telecommunications market in the second half of the 1990s. In the first month after its launch, Esat Digifone acquired 11,000 subscribers. When we went on to launch the Speakeasy mobile phone service, it outsold the competition by three to one and acquired a 23% market share within six weeks. Esat Telecom saw its corporate customer base grow to 6,000 and won contracts with the biggest multinational companies based in Ireland.

We always believed that Esat would succeed in the long run, but its success far exceeded our expectations. We thought we might build a company worth $100 million. We came close to that in June 1996, having given away 50% to investors. I remember sharing privately my surprise that we had come so far with my associate Paul Connolly. We had thought $100 million was the beginning of the end.

The initial public offering (IPO) was a sure sign that Esat had acquired international credibility and investor confidence in future growth potential. In advance of the IPO, we launched a European and US roadshow to whet the appetite of investors. The roadshow team visited seventy fund managers in seven European cities over five days. The US roadshow trail covered an even greater number of accounts in thirteen cities. After just one week of the European roadshow, with the US marketing yet to come, the interest in shares showed that the IPO would be oversubscribed. In October 1997 we launched Esat on the Nasdaq Stock Market at a share price of $13, valuing us at $220 million. We went on to make a secondary share offering in June 1998 that valued the company at $400 million.

Takeover

Within two years, Esat had grown so strongly that, ultimately, when our Esat Digifone partners made a hostile bid for the entire Esat company at $75 per share, I dismissed it as a major undervaluation of the company. When they increased their offer to $85 per share, I was still adamant that Esat was worth more. I set up a 'white knight' team to target the interest of other potential takeover candidates who might 'rescue' us from the hostile takeover bid. Tony Belinkoff of investment bank Donaldson, Lufkin & Jenrette joined Paul Connolly, Massimo Prelz of Advent International and me on the team. British Telecom suddenly stepped into the arena and declared an interest in negotiating.

I flew to London with Paul Connolly, and we were secretively picked up by a car at our hotel to be driven to an undisclosed British Telecom office. All the way to the meeting venue, Paul and I role-played our negotiating strategy. We agreed a series of prompts that would trigger each other's arguments during the meeting. We arrived in the car-park basement of a building and were brought by lift to a boardroom to meet the top British Telecom executives and their legal and financial advisors. The role-play preparation paid dividends, because we even staged a feigned walkout from the meeting when we felt their bid price was too low. At this point, British Telecom's finance director put out his hand and asked us to keep our seats. At that moment I knew we had a potential deal in sight. On 6 January 2000, British Telecom agreed to buy Esat Telecom at a price of $100 per share, or $2.46 billion for the entire company.

At the time of the sale to British Telecom in January 2000, the industry environment was ripe for us. We had talented people who created value in a bull market that placed faith in the telecom sector. We looked closely at comparative valuations of other second national telecom companies and realized that we were ahead on comparative measurements but behind on valuation. Suddenly, the goal was to kill the poor image that some Irish publicly quoted companies had acquired and to bury any sense of non-delivery. There was strong international interest in our shares, and we said, 'We're going absolutely, single-mindedly to make as much for shareholders as possible and show what we can do.' There was a passion to not let the side down and to nail the highest sale value, whatever it took. We 'roadshowed' continuously to deliver our story and boost investor confidence. I recall spending St Stephen's Day with Paul Connolly phoning our US investors to keep them in the ruck in advance of the British Telecom white knight bid. It was a signal to our investors that we were working every day to get the best price.

The Irish are famous for eloquence and creativity, but in the not-too-distant past we were not taken seriously as business people. I believe that the likes of Michael O'Leary, Chris Horn and a new stratum of business leaders have managed to improve faith in Irish enterprise dramatically. By ensuring we received maximum value from the sale of Esat to BT for our shareholders, we played our part also. We can be happy with Esat's success, but we honestly didn't know how it was going to work out. It was an adventure from the start. It was like the searching for the right path in the Spencer Tracey movie *Northwest Passage* – we knew where we wanted to go but had to venture into the unknown to find the path.

Enterprise excitement . . .

There is something exciting about launching into the unknown, but more specifically, there is something exciting about launching businesses. I get more from launching a business than running one. I certainly have a reasonably good ability to run a large company and very much enjoy that, but give me a start-up any day and the adrenaline starts to pump.

The start-up feeling is extraordinary. When you bring new people together and gather around one table to decide the direction, shape and nature of a business, an energy is unleashed that is both unusual and exciting. Our Jamaican experience is a great example. We have twelve Irish people on the team launching the Digicell mobile network. They are currently in the middle of the start-up phase with a lot of major issues to resolve, from creating the infrastructure to hiring and training local staff. The obstacles we face are like elements of a large puzzle. There is a tremendous buzz from employing collective intelligence, wit and determination to solve it. When people have experienced several start-ups, they can identify and overcome the obstacles more quickly. It is important to me to be a central part of the start-up. It is not just another investment 6,000 miles away. I travel there every two weeks to listen to what the team has to say. Leslie Buckley and I fly in there in the morning, fly out in the evening and arrive back in London within a day. The effort is worth it to show clearly my interest and support, as well as monitoring performance.

. . . and struggle

The day that is in it is an interesting one. It has been a rare day of reflection on the past and what we have been lucky enough to achieve. This morning at 7.30 I walked into our new offices here on Grand Canal Quay. I looked around me and said, 'This is unbelievable. This is a long way from meagre beginnings in Mount Street. But is this a good thing or a bad thing? Will it lead to a loss of reality?' I don't think it will, but it is certainly salubrious, and I have yet to get comfortable with that. The furniture in my old office all came from Century Radio's liquidation sale. It is good to remember that the line is thin between success and failure. It is only very recently that we have had any real money to play with, and the contrast is interesting. If given the choice of which side of the line I would rather be on, I would find it hard to choose. I like the struggle. I could easily adjust to having few means. In reflective moments I sometimes pine for my life of five to seven years ago. I wonder if the excitement of the struggle is greater than the satisfaction of achievement. Some people say that the struggle is self-fulfilling. Running from one crisis to another is addictive, but you can end up being caught in that crisis existence for the rest of your life.

There are plenty of outstanding small-business people who have been struggling for twenty years. These people are the backbone of the economy. Although they lack the huge wealth or the high profile, their efforts are as heroic and their ability as great as those more fortunate by circumstance. What they have missed, perhaps, is the good fortune and the right circumstances to 'make it'. I have seen many good ventures go under as a result of such bad luck as a turn in exchange rates, for instance.

Certainly, more people are undertaking enterprise ventures now than 15 years ago. I see two reasons for this. Firstly, more money is in circulation from several sources. People are realizing the value of their share options, venture capital is accessible and property inheritance has a greater value. The more money there is, the less fear there is of losing it. Secondly, people are more prepared to accept failure now. Fifteen years ago, failure was accompanied by a heavy black mark, whereas people discard any such inhibitions now and forgiveness comes more easily. I firmly believe that is a good thing.

Ideals and values

One consequence of working from 7 a.m. until 9 p.m. has been a lack of time to pursue outside interests. However, I have always had a strong interest in human rights. Recently I initiated a human rights defence trust, 'Frontline', with the former director of Amnesty International in Ireland, Mary Lawlor. Frontline seeks to extract activists from situations that have suddenly become dangerous to their welfare or lives. Many corporate people have an unfortunate image of the activists working in organizations such as Greenpeace and Amnesty International. They see the activists as a thorn in the side and a constraint on progressive business, which is of course untrue. They don't realize the extent to which other parts of the world have a different culture and philosophy and a different system of social organization and government. I hope that this trust initiative can be a source of some education.

I am very interested in education. My hero is Joe O'Toole, senator and president of the Irish National Teachers' Organisation. I think that the Department of Education is living on former years of glory and must move on from old ways of thinking. Teachers are every bit as important as doctors and dentists, and they should be paid accordingly. Classrooms of thirty-four children should be a thing of the past. Schoolbags should be filled with educational goodies, such as a personal computer. Getting every child typing at the age of six is the only way to bring underprivileged communities to a par with the privileged. Every child should have the opportunity to develop computer proficiency, or a new poverty of information will emerge within a two-tier society made up of those who have access to information and its benefits and those who do not.

I would pay teachers better wages, linked to performance and results. I would put a computer in every student's hands and bring broader bandwidth into schools for speed and volume of information. I would support more science initiatives such as the Young Scientists Exhibition. These improvements must happen, but the problem in this country is that nobody sits up on a roof and gets a bin lid out to move things up a gear.

I was never involved in student politics in college. I could never make any money from it, and I needed funds at the time. I had a choice in college. I could get involved in student politics, or I could go and paint a house or an office and support my lifestyle.

Tastes and culture

I love 98FM. It is a fantastic cutting-edge business because it works in real time. If you play two bad records in a row, all your listeners will leave. Consumer tastes are changing continually. Every week 98FM does research by interviewing 200 to 300 listeners, both individually and in auditorium sessions. Consumer research is crucial because it drives the

production wheel forward. Research creates good programming that captures an audience, drives advertising and brings
in the revenue.

I think that young people especially have become far more
sophisticated in their tastes. I am glad that the very insular,
protectionist policies of the 1930s and 1940s are far behind us.
Seán Lemass, Jack Lynch and Garret FitzGerald cultivated an
openness that has allowed Ireland to flourish, and young
people have developed a worldly sophistication. Trends and
tastes are heavily influenced by two distinct cultures – a flash
US culture of video games and MTV and a slightly more staid
European culture. In terms of which of these cultures will have
the greater influence, Ireland is at a crossroads.

My advice to those who embrace the enterprise culture: start
small and modest. Understand the simplicity of buying and
selling. If you can buy for a pound and sell for two, you are in
business. An idea does not have to be sophisticated. There's
nothing wrong with washing cars to compete with the local
garage. Unfortunately, that kind of enterprise culture is a little
blunted, because people don't like getting their hands dirty. I
would encourage any child of mine to try hands-on jobs like
waiting or waitressing. Learning about human nature in a
hands-on environment is fantastic. It will remove any shyness
and foster both a service and a selling mentality. It's part of the
education of life.

PÁDRAIG Ó CÉIDIGH

Managing director/co-owner, Aer Árann;

Founder, Foinse newspaper

*P*ádraig Ó Céidigh was born in Spiddal in County Galway, where he still lives with his wife, Caitlín, and their four children, Emer, Cathal, Tríona and Fáinse, a stone's throw away from his first home. Born into a bilingual family with an ethos for hard work, he has succeeded in enterprise through determination and fearlessness.

He completed a Jesuit education in Coláiste Iognáid in Galway and attended University College Galway to study for a bachelor's degree in commerce. After graduation, he started an accounting career with KPMG in Limerick. Restlessness in a deskbound job set his aspirations drifting after only one year, and when his old school headmaster, Fr Tyrell, approached him and asked him if he would consider becoming a teacher, he grasped the opportunity to switch careers. Pádraig taught for several years in Coláiste Iognáid and developed a passion for creating a learning environment for his students. While teaching, he undertook law studies by night in UCG and qualified as a solicitor. He finally diverted his energy from teaching to starting his own legal practice in Galway city, as well as a series of enterprise ventures that included a small computer company and a printing service.

Pádraig's love of the Irish language led him to launch an Irish-language newspaper, Foinse, which has grown to become Ireland's biggest-selling Irish-language newspaper. In 1994, an opportunity *arose to take on a business challenge for which his appetite had been whetted. With the aid of a friend, he purchased the airline that serviced the Aran Islands, Aer Árann, and has since upgraded its fleet and services to the status of a national carrier that shuttles commuters from the regions to the capital on a daily basis. He has also turned his hand to presentation on both television and radio. He manages an Irish-language school and a music school in Galway. Such diversity of enterprise is reflected in his favourite sayings: 'Change brings challenge' and 'I'd give it a go – why not?' His positive attitude is contagious. He believes that anything is possible, and his story bears testament.*

Taking over Aer Árann

I had flown only a handful of times with Aer Árann, which operated flights from Galway to the Aran Islands only, before I became intrigued by the nature of its operations. I knew very little about the aviation industry at the time, but I had an instinctive feeling that there was great room for improvement in the efficiency of this small airline's operations. I recall thinking to myself in passing that if ever the opportunity arose, Aer Árann could be transformed into a rewarding business. In 1994, the company, which was then under the stewardship of Tim Kilroe, was put up for sale, and my interest was rekindled. I could not raise sufficient personal loans from the banks to meet the asking price. While golfing one afternoon with Eugene O'Kelly, an anaesthetist in Galway, I mentioned to him that there was this little airline called Aer Árann up for sale. Eugene knew hardly anything about the company. I asked him if he would be interested in helping me to buy it. He reflected for a week and replied that he would love to get involved. He agreed to invest if I would run the company. We designed a 50–50 partnership, and I prepared a strategy to run the company after our purchase. I had little interest in aeroplanes. I saw Aer Árann purely in terms of its business potential. It is in the business of transportation, just like a car hire, bus or train company. I did not have a deep knowledge of aviation, but I did not need to have all the knowledge or skills required. I do not have to fly or fix the aeroplanes. I just run the business.

I inherited a rich legacy when I took over Aer Árann. The history of Aer Árann started in 1969 with a letter from Colie Hernon, cox of the Inishmore lifeboat, to the *Connacht Tribune*, suggesting that an air link would save time in medical emergencies. On 15 August 1970, the Minister for the Gaeltacht, Mr Michael Kitt, officially launched the first route between Inishmore and the mainland. That same night a storm blew, and Aer Árann's first and only aeroplane, an Islander EI-AUL, which was parked dangerously close to the water's edge on Inishmore, became unsettled in the high winds. Several of the island's strongest men, toasting the launch of the airline in their local hostelry, were coaxed into bracing the elements and acted as ballast for the Islander until the winds subsided. Aer Árann has experienced a stormy passage ever since that night. The airline was losing significant money by the mid-1970s until an American multimillionaire, John Mulcahy, invested sufficient funds to keep the business afloat. By 1980, however, the airline was in financial trouble once more, and closure seemed imminent. Roscommon-born Tim Kilroe, owner of the Manchester-based Air Kilroe, purchased the airline outright from Mulcahy and injected new life into the company. In the mid-1980s, Aer Árann won several licences to operate regional and cross-channel flights. With the exception of a short-lived Dublin–Shannon service, the licences were never exploited, and the airline reverted to servicing the Aran Islands and depending on a swell of summer tourist traffic for survival.

I had a very basic business philosophy for Aer Árann. Firstly, I set out to capture more of the available market of people travelling to the Aran Islands. I recognized that there were more than 1 million people visiting Galway each year. One-quarter of these travelled to the Aran Islands by boat. I knew that if I could convert just 5% of that 250,000 to flying to the Islands, I would more than double my income. I invested in a big marketing campaign in the greater Galway area, where billboard signs advertised our flight deals to the Islands. Within one season, the number of passengers flying to the Aran Islands doubled.

Secondly, I wanted to increase income by reducing costs. To facilitate this, I decided to let three senior managers of Aer Árann go. There was a young girl called Marie Mulrooney, who did not have a significant role in the company at that time and who I believed had a wealth of untapped potential. I asked her if she would become the manager of the company. I told her that I would support her at every step, and she accepted the offer. Together we set out to strip away inefficiencies and grow in size and depth. Within two years, I had paid off all my initial bank loans and then raised a further £250,000 for developing our runways, of which £100,000 was a government investment.

Growing business

There were two ways in which I could expand the business. We could become Ireland's premier island airline company, or we could compete on internal routes in Ireland. The first option would require the building of airstrips on other islands. This would have required political support. The government invests in airstrips in the same way that they invest in road infrastructure. The political support was not strong enough to make it happen at the time, so I looked to expanding inland. I explored other airline models around the world, particularly in Europe. I saw that British Airways, KLM and Air France were changing their own strategies in the way they did business. Instead of being all things to all people and flying every route they could, they were focussing on international travel and using smaller airlines to cover the less lucrative routes. These small airlines would feed passengers into their international hub from peripheral areas and develop a franchise relationship with them. I foresaw that Aer Lingus would soon follow this strategy and need a small airline to feed passengers into its Dublin and Shannon hubs. With over 7,000 employees, Aer Lingus was not suited to providing an internal air service in Ireland.

In 1995, I started creating a model airline to suit the internal market in Ireland. My objective was to provide a feeder service for Aer Lingus or any other airline operating international flights out of Ireland. Three years ago, I made an application to the Department of Public Enterprise, which administers what is called the Public Service Obligation (PSO) route contracts. These are three-year contracts with grant aid for a European airline to provide a service from the regions into and out of Dublin. I had only two nine-seat aeroplanes in Connemara at the time of the application, and the contract required operation of fifty-seat aeroplanes. Aer Lingus won the contract, but we ran them very close to the wire. The loss of this contract opportunity was a benchmark for me, and it allowed me to develop a strategy and a thought process to really go for it next time round. I look back on the failure to win as a trial run.

I grew in respect for the professional manner in which the Department of Public Enterprise ran the contract applications. Despite not winning the contract, we began a solid and good relationship with the Department, based on a positive and upfront approach. It is unfortunate that many people default to a clichéd criticism of civil servants and department officials. They are really fine people, and we are very fortunate to have civil servants of their calibre in Ireland.

In 1998, an airline called Ireland Airways, which had the PSO contract to fly between Dublin and Donegal, went bust. When the Department of Public Enterprise advertised that contract, I was eager and waiting for the opportunity to apply, and we won the contract. That contract required an aeroplane with nineteen seats minimum. Initially, I thought a Jetstream 31 aeroplane, which has nineteen passenger seats, would be sufficient. However, when I looked more closely at the potential of the Donegal market to grow, I decided to change the business model and procure a Shorts 360 aeroplane with thirty-six passenger seats.

I approached an airline called BAC Express, based in Gatwick. They operated a Shorts 360 aeroplane, which they were flying between Dublin and the Isle of Man. I examined their market and operations and the utilization of their aeroplane and concluded that they were not capturing the full value from the Shorts 360 as a resource. The plane was on the ground too much of the time. I discussed this with them, and they suggested that I lease the plane for use on my Donegal route. I replied that I would take both their aeroplane and the route together. With a little persuasion, they agreed. I launched the Donegal route and flew to the Isle of Man with the one aeroplane. In addition, I undertook a freight contract and flew the same aeroplane back and forth to Coventry at night. By using my resource to the maximum in this way, breaking even came swiftly and easily.

No finance? No problem

At the beginning of that year, Aer Árann in Dublin consisted of one person on a mobile phone sitting on an orange box in the middle of arrivals in Dublin airport. He was our reservations man, our reception, our accountant, our marketing manager and our financial controller. Now we have 170 full-time people and up to 50 part-time and contracting people working for us. We essentially created something out of nothing when we took over Aer Árann. We had minimal funding when we undertook this growth. Money is not the lifeblood of a business. Belief and passion in your objectives are the essentials. You have to truly believe in what you are doing and where you are going. If you do not, nobody else will. Forcing belief and passion on other people does not work. If you force yourself on another, they are inclined to take a step back. Progression is made through demonstrating belief and passion in everything you do and convincing people to act likewise.

In 2000, we took the next step in our growth strategy and applied for a series of PSO contracts throughout the country. On 17 December 2000, the Department of Public Enterprise informed us that we had been awarded five of the six national PSO contracts. I was thrilled with this stamp of approval on our services and excited about the prospect of growth ahead. We would now be flying the routes to Donegal, Sligo, Knock, Galway and Kerry out of Dublin. To fulfil our contract obligations, I needed to have five aeroplanes operating the routes by early February 2001. An immediate injection of £3 million for new aeroplanes was needed. Furthermore, I had to train pilots at a cost of £500,000. I did not have that money in place and spent all of Christmas struggling to find a solution. I devised a plan that did not require raising the money from a lending institution or selling a stake in Aer Árann. I paid a visit to the manufacturer of the ATR-42, which is the type of fifty-seat aeroplane I had selected to use. ATR is the biggest manufacturer of turboprop aircraft in the world. I sat down in front of the president of ATR in his office in Paris. He had a big map of Europe on his wall and a couple of small French flags on his desk. He agreed to provide the aeroplanes and train my pilots but insisted on full payment in advance. I told him that I did not have the money but could make the payment after operations had broken even. He replied that he would like to help me but could not do so without upfront payment. I leant over his desk, took one of his French flags and stuck it in Dublin on his map. I said, 'Look here, do you want that flag in Dublin? If you do, I can get it there for you. But man, you have to put your hand across the table and dance with me. If you do, it will happen. If you don't, so be it, it will not happen.' To that, he replied, 'Interesting Irish man!' and then he put out his hand. We struck a deal to scupper the advance payment and arranged a reasonable monthly lease. I was able to fulfil the contract requirements and deadlines. When the PSO contracts end in three years time, I will be in an even stronger position to re-apply for them with start-up costs out of the way. The new regional routes have not diverted our attention from the roots of our business. We have continued to strengthen our services to the Aran Islands and fly to all three of the Islands up to twenty-five times daily through the summer months.

Good people

I have superb staff. They would spill blood for the team. People are the greatest asset a business can have. Aer Árann people have a sense of integrity and trust and believe in our shared objectives. Six months after I took over the company, one of the engines of our aeroplane blew out. To stay flying and in business, we needed another engine, which would cost £20,000. The staff knew I did not have the money and that the company would be in serious trouble without an operating aeroplane. Two of the staff approached me and offered to provide the £20,000 for a new engine, allowing the company to pay them back when it could. That is an example of the remarkable commitment at Aer Árann.

When I interview a prospective staff team member, I look not only at the skills that somebody can bring to the company but also at how they can develop as individuals within the company. I intuitively explore what they can learn in the company. I also assess if there is sufficient space in a candidate to learn and grow, as well as a willingness to allow that space to be expanded. I need people who are happy to push the limits of their comfort and stretch themselves. I need good people who are sometimes willing to walk down a dark road, not knowing what is at the end of it.

Good human communication is essential to Aer Árann. The company revolves around building strong relationships within the company and with our customers and various stakeholders. We endeavour to work positively together and develop together. There is a diversity of people at Aer Árann that contributes to a learning environment. The most successful learning companies have embraced diversity, integrating, in particular, the male and female thought processes, which are complementary. Differences between men and women in business are positive. The team of staff at Aer Árann work with me, rather than for me, and that is a distinction that is important. Quality of service and operation is also highly important to me. We are the first European airline to receive the ISO9000 award. The award promotes the recognition of our quality, safety and reliability – important attributes to any passenger. ISO9000 also facilitated the introduction of new systems and structures in the company that will act as a foundation for future growth. Marie Mulrooney, Mary Gilmore and Gráinne Flaherty were the three managers that led the drive to win the ISO9000 award. The commitment and spirit that they instilled in Aer Árann in the process would have been worthwhile even in the event of not receiving the award. They created a sense that while individuals can do so much, collective action can achieve an awful lot more.

Education and enterprise

Chris Horn, of IONA Technologies, and I addressed a gathering of Irish university academics at a conference in Malahide in 1999. The conference aimed to provoke a debate on the role of education in meeting the skills needs of Irish industry. In the provocative and challenging spirit of the gathering, I suggested that Irish educational institutions are providing a product for a society that no longer exists. Ireland has an academic curriculum with roots that extend sixty years into the past. I am forty-three, and my children are being taught the same way that I was taught when I was at school. My parents did not go beyond primary education, but people of their vintage who did attend secondary school were taught in generally the same way that I was taught. Despite the advent of computers and multimedia tools, teaching philosophy has not evolved. Students are taught what to learn but not how to learn. Some teachers strive to be pioneers in the educational system, but they are few in number and are seen as mavericks.

I too was probably seen as a maverick when I was a teacher.

I taught mathematics and accountancy to students in Coláiste Iognáid in Galway for six years. I really enjoyed the challenge of teaching. I soon discovered that 'teaching' was an inaccurate term for what I felt I was doing. I believed that my purpose was not to teach but to facilitate learning, and there is a fundamental difference between the two. I tried to create an environment in which students would be relaxed and receptive, so that they could absorb information easily, quickly and effortlessly. I wanted them to learn in the same way that somebody instinctively learns how to ride a bicycle or drive a car. Once you can ride one bicycle, you can ride any bicycle. If I could successfully teach them how a mind learns, they would be able to learn any subject of their choosing.

A good friend of mine, Brendan Colleran, once gave me a present of a book in return for helping him to put together a business plan for a canoeing business. The book made a deep impact on me. It was called *Creative Visualization* and was written by a lady named Shakti Gawain. I had to read it about three times before I could understand what it meant. It describes how to use personal creativity to achieve objectives. I wondered how I could use this to help my students to do better and to use their creativity to learn? I began to read more and more books on related subjects such as cognitive science and the science of learning. I learnt about the right and left sides of the brain and how memory is shaped and functions.

I started to develop my own model of teaching based on what I was learning. Without deviating radically from the traditional methods of teaching, I introduced new tools and techniques in the classroom. For instance, I asked my students to write their own Leaving Certificate mathematics book while using the standard academic texts as back-up. In writing their own books, they fashioned their very own personal set of notes. The books were their personal creations, with whatever colours or highlights that were most appropriate to their learning needs and styles. My students agreed that their personal textbooks were much more meaningful to them. I wondered how the authors of the standard textbooks could know what each of my students needed. Many authors had experienced different teaching conditions and environments and certainly never taught the students in my class. I believe that every student is different. Each is a unique individual, so I developed a unique learning strategy with each one. I believe the strategies were very successful. My classes had very few discipline problems, the students enjoyed coming to class, and they achieved good results.

Out of interest, I started to study law by night at UCG, and I began teaching law to my transition-year students. We were one of the first schools in Ireland to teach law. It has been taught to O-level students in the United Kingdom for thirty years. I wanted my students to learn about the fundamental principles of law, the rules that govern the sale of goods, consumer rights and the Irish Constitution. I ran into difficulties with some of my fellow teachers, who thought I was deviating too much from traditional subjects and teaching methods. I felt under constant pressure to conform to the established teaching frameworks. The contradiction between the urge to conform and the need to maintain my difference became a large source of mental conflict. I began to feel that if I remained a teacher, I would be a hypocrite because I would be working in a straitjacketed system that did not operate in the best interests of the students. It did not encourage creativity, and most teachers were not willing to accept change and try something different. One day I came home from school, and my wife, Caitlín, and I went for a walk, and she said, 'Look, take a career break', so I did.

After leaving teaching, I knew that I did not want to go back to accounting, so I decided to set up a law practice. I initially set up my practice at home, but when the business grew, I moved to Galway city. At this time, I had set up a music school in Galway city with a friend of mine, Carl Hession, which was going well, and I took over one of the rooms to use as an office. The practice went very well, and in order to build up the business further, I decided to contact Raidió na Gaeltachta for publicity. I suggested to them that they might start a phone-in programme for people to air legal queries that I would answer live on radio. They agreed to the idea straight away. I turned down an offer of payment for my time because it was pure enjoyment and an excellent advertisement that generated a lot of new client business for my practice. Despite the fact that the practice was going well, I found that there were areas of law in which I was weak. I didn't like it. Furthermore, I felt frustrated at the concept of being tied to a desk. I prefer to be out meeting people and at the centre of the action. I started to play with a few other business ideas. I started a printing company, launched an Irish-language newspaper, *Foinse*, ran Irish-language colleges and started a computer company with my brother. It was at this time that I got involved in Aer Árann. For some two years, I ran the law firm and Aer Árann alongside each other until I eventually closed the practice to devote more time to Aer Árann.

I could not have maintained so many business interests without the support I got at home. Because of the ease I feel at home with my wife and children, I am able to concentrate on business projects, and Caitlín has always been a rock of support to me. She has always believed in me. If I decided to try a new business venture, she would back me up, and that gave me a great confidence and comfort. I could not have done anything without her.

Foinse *and the Irish language*

When I set up *Foinse*, I knew nothing about newspapers. I launched my own newspaper because I was disillusioned with the way the Irish language was written in established newspapers. They lacked imagination and originality. Many Irish-language journalists had an embittered and negative attitude to the media and the government. I wanted to create something positive – something different. I wanted to create a medium in which young people with fresh ideas and without prejudice could express themselves in the Irish language. *Foinse* means 'source' in English, and I hoped that this paper would be a source of positive expression of life in contemporary Ireland. I am a very visual person, and I like building models on blank pages. I sketched the form of *Foinse* and became more enthusiastic as the model took shape. I decided to launch the paper from Carraroe, in the heart of Connemara. We now have reached sales of 10,000 copies a week – more than any Irish-language newspaper in history. I have little interest in the money generated from the newspaper. The thrilling sense of achievement is what drives me.

I am delighted to be able to promote the Irish language and be part of what I see as a revival of interest. Former minister Michael D. Higgins has been a visionary in promoting the language. I have no political favourites, but I think the introduction of the Irish-language television station, TG4, under Michael D. Higgins has played an enormous role in modernizing the Irish language and spreading it throughout the nation. In 2000, I became involved in presenting a live show on TG4, called *Ardán*, which is the Irish for 'stage' or 'platform'. I had never been on television before in my life, but I had a go because it was there to be done, and I enjoyed it hugely. Raidió na Gaeltachta has also played a role in promoting the modern language widely, and I believe that *Foinse* contributes in terms of the written word. Many Irish-language organizations have yet to join this modernism and are still presenting an image of the language that is entrenched in the 1950s and not the new century. The one aspect that bothers me about the Irish language is the way the Gaeltacht areas have been fashioned in people's minds as Indian reservations – accorded a sense of isolation and viewed with indifference. I think Irish is for everyone and the culture is for everyone. People decide subjectively how much they want to immerse themselves in it, but I hope they embrace the culture and language as an inherent part of Irish life. The language is ultimately in the hands of young people. If city social clubs such as Sult in Dublin and Irish cafés established throughout the country are an example to judge by, the future is bright.

West and home

Young people living in the Gaeltacht areas have changed an awful lot in recent years. A new cosmopolitan attitude is evident. They believe they are on an equal footing with anybody, anywhere in the world, and they have a huge new sense of self-confidence. That confidence has inspired young people to try their hand at novel enterprises. Making a success of an enterprise in the West is tough. Enterprises outside Dublin are hampered mainly by problems of accessibility. Telecommunications and broadband technology can help to overcome access restrictions, and this suits particular types of enterprises, but a business needs efficient physical access also. This is part of the strategy that I want to pursue with Aer Árann. I want to go as close as I can to creating a shuttle service between Dublin and the regions that is like a bus in the sky. I want people to be able to get a ticket and hop off and on a commuter service.

To relax or unwind, I run. In 1999 I ran the New York City marathon. I had planned to run the 2000 marathon but instead was presenting the programme, *Ardán*, from Castlebar. I run between 5 and 8 miles three nights every week. I love walking or jogging in the rain or going down to the beach on my own for an hour or two in the evenings. I organize mini-marathons on the Aran Islands for which 100 participants raise £500 each to donate to Our Lady's Hospital for Sick Children in Crumlin, Dublin. In total we raised £100,000 for the hospital this year. The funds will be used to buy a cardiac unit for children who have to travel to London to have access to this equipment. I have four kids, and, thank God, they are all healthy, but I know people who have not been so fortunate. The most important stage in my own life was my childhood, when I learnt a huge amount from growing up in Co. Galway. From the age of nine or ten, I spent weekends picking periwinkles on the beach near home and sold them to pay for my first watch, my first bicycle and my first momentous trip to Dublin. Today, I fly back and forth between Galway and Dublin on my own airline to be in time for dinner at home with my family, only today I am not eating periwinkles.

PAT & ANNETTE SHANAHAN

CEO, Tellabs Ireland;

Vice-president, Tellabs International

Clinic director, Abbey Physio;

Lecturer, Royal College of Surgeons

*O*n a wintry morning, I stepped from a train in Limerick city station and was greeted warmly by Pat Shanahan. He drove me across the wide Shannon to his home. There, safe from the elements and cheered by the friendly banter and good food, I chatted with Annette and Pat Shanahan about their individual enterprises, their love of family and the work–life balance they have achieved.

Pat's uncle was one of Ireland's most famous and celebrated hurling goalkeepers, Paddy Scanlan of Limerick. Today, Annette is the chartered physiotherapist for the Limerick county hurling teams – an enjoyable diversion from her many enterprise activities. This happy coincidence is only one example of the way in which they complement each other perfectly. They have supported each other's business ambitions while maintaining a secure family environment. They have achieved a sense of unity as a family without compromising the individuality that has allowed them to excel in their respective enterprises. It is this sense of completion that makes their story so appealing.

Young lives

Pat: A truly formative part of my young working life was the nine months I spent working in India. I was working for an engineering company, Marconi, installing equipment in Russian fighter jets. India was exciting and inspiring. The vibrancy, the colour and the culture were fascinating, but the poverty, the suffering and the social deprivation were shocking. I found the relation of the caste system and the whiteness of the skin to societal status and affluence intriguing. My experience in India, half a world away from my home in Limerick, brought me a new awareness and perspective. When I returned from India, I had a greater sense of what was important in life to me, and I felt a sense of privilege, which has never left me. I feel that the good education and opportunities that I have been afforded have given me the ability to effectively control my own destiny – a self-determination enjoyed by few.

My mother had qualified in London as a state-registered nurse, and my father was an electrician. Both instilled in me an ethos of hard work, and my father, who had a natural ability in mathematics and science, was not only a great help with homework but generated a natural interest in power and electrical devices. His fascination in listening to the BBC World Service on the radio meant that he was a mine of information, which he shared at the slightest show of interest. My mother assisted the local doctor on many a delivery, and Annette still has patients from the area declaring their connection with my mother's care – a sort of continuation of care by the females in the family.

The work ethic I learnt from my parents was also acquired during many an early morning, mopping the floors of our family pub, Scanlan's, in Castleconnell, Limerick. As in any family business, I learnt that you had to pull together and share the workload to sustain a living. As I was an only child, it was expected that I would eventually take over the reins and run the pub. However, the pub business was not for me, and my parents were supportive when I announced that I had other plans for the future. I decided to study electronic engineering at University College Cork. I believed the degree would be a passport to the world. After graduation I emigrated to England, where I began my work with Marconi, which ultimately sent me to India.

My early work involved designing an array of electronic components. I very quickly began to understand how to realize the potential of these components in novel ways to create new products that addressed market needs. Soon I moved up the food chain to a position of managing other designers. I added an important commercial outlook to my focus on engineering design as I grew in experience. I enjoyed talking to customers, a skill I fashioned at an early stage in life with plenty of experience in the pub at home, listening for many hours to customers, hoping to get to the punchline and interpreting exactly what people wanted, or at least convincing them that what I came up with was what they wanted. These may not always be one and the same thing, but you hope to achieve as close a fit as possible. In my engineering work, I had to understand different customer requirements and communicate these to the engineers who would build the products.

I left Marconi to work for Westinghouse in Shannon, which afforded the right opportunity to return to Ireland. A tax break for returning immigrants was an added incentive, something well worth revisiting in the present day to attract home the level of expertise needed to sustain our growing economy. I recall this incentive paid for a new car at the time.

I was beginning to settle back in Limerick, playing rugby and enjoying the social life for which Limerick is renowned. I found Limerick to be a rejuvenated city, with many people from Ireland and around the world making a home in the city and creating a new atmosphere of diversity and industry. Limerick was also building a reputation as a respected centre of learning, with the excellent University of Limerick and Institute of Technology that have grown in strength with every passing year. I have often heard reference to Limerick as Ireland's best-kept secret. Our media image is often far removed from the reality, although there is always much to improve. I met Annette in Limerick at one of many hospital parties I attended. I knew I had met someone special from the first word, and I believe there was many a pint cried over at our surprise engagement party. Within a year of meeting, we were married, and only one year away from our twentieth anniversary, there are no regrets.

At the age of twenty-nine, I had a secure job in a safe company when the chance arose to join a volatile telecommunications operation called Mitel, in Shannon. Mitel had been experiencing difficult times because of growth-related problems. The opportunity was still great for future growth, but the accompanying risk was equally great, and the company's future was indeed unclear. My decision to renege on stability caused me some heartache, but ultimately, I was drawn by the excitement of the growth potential in a more enterprising environment, and I joined Mitel feeling daunted but hopeful.

Annette: I had been working as a chartered physiotherapist in the Regional Hospital in Limerick. Although my parents are Irish, I was born and raised in England, so coming to Ireland was a sort of homecoming. I first studied physiotherapy in Nottingham, and at the age of twenty-one, I was drawn to the capital. London was bright and full of life and naturally attracted me with its energy. To live on a physiotherapist's salary in London, even in the early 1980s, and have any chance of saving enough money for a house was pretty impossible, so I took a short but lucrative career break in recruitment. I quickly developed good people- and organization-management skills and was promoted to senior management. I learnt as much as I could in a management role so that I could apply this later to the activities I wanted to pursue – enterprise and my own business. I kick-started my learning in enterprise in London by buying property at the onset of the property boom, renovating it and selling it at a higher price. My renovation skills were mainly in interior decorating. I bought good second-hand furniture that I sourced from local newspaper 'articles for sale' advertise- ments or notices in local post offices. I still have some of those bargain buys. It was at a time when many people were throwing out their heirloom furniture in favour of the more modern G-Plan and Ercol ranges with a woodgrain effect. Ironically, this type of heirloom furniture is now undergoing a revival as a 'retro' fashion. I let the properties, usually to friends, and when I finally sold them, property prices had soared. This gave me the financial security to continue in physiotherapy and to start my own business at a young age. My mother was a big influence on me. She had been doing interior decorating for many years. My father was a builder and was delighted when I arrived home to announce that I had made my first property purchase, though surprised I had not consulted him. He was supportive of his headstrong eldest, giving me just enough slack in the rope to make mistakes, none of which were irrevocable but all of which were big enough to learn from. When he died suddenly at forty-eight years of age, I was the only one of five children to have finished college or school. My mother has been an exceptional woman, both as our Mum, and as 'M.D.' of the 'family firm'. She has overcome many difficulties in her life with dignity and faith. A lady before her time, she has a wealth of opinions on the contribution of women to society. She is my role model and presides over the growing family as a matriarch.

After I had come to live in Limerick and with the support of Pat, I started my chartered physiotherapy practice. We sacrificed part of our home and bought the equipment I needed. My intention had always been to expand the practice to meet a growing demand, and this soon outstripped my resources at home. I moved to premises in town, and the practice soon employed six physiotherapists, an occupational health and safety consultant and two administration staff. At this stage, I decided that I was involved with an enterprise more than purely a practice and sought new ways to expand. In liaison with the University of Limerick and the Royal College of Surgeons in Dublin, we undertook research projects that not only raised the profile of the clinic but also provided clinical placements for students, giving them a chance to learn in a professional environment. The Royal College of Surgeons now invites me to give a series of lectures in occupational health to students each year, and the University of Limerick has also asked me to lecture.

When I started the physiotherapy practice, both Pat and I had big hopes for each of our individual areas of enterprise. To achieve these hopes, we each gave the other huge support and encouragement. In fact, we drew up what we called our 'five-year plan'. We could never have known how well it might work out. We knew that this would be our family time as well, and we had three fantastic children – Claire, Fiona and Rory.

Buy-out opportunity

Pat: I certainly felt Annette's support through those years. Six months after I joined Mitel, I was promoted to plant manager. I believed strongly that I could help to turn the troubled plant around and overcome its problems of overstretching due to growth. However, shortly afterwards, Mitel decided to pull out of Ireland, and it seemed that the carpet was being pulled from beneath us. At thirty, I was young and confident and had always wanted to succeed at enterprise on my own, so I approached the Mitel senior officers with a plan to complete a management buy-out of the company. With the help of a business consultant, Bob Holder, who remains a close friend and colleague to this day, and three management colleagues, we set about developing a business plan. The excitement of taking the company into our own hands grew stronger with every passing day. I really believed that we could make the company a success without Mitel and was energized by the challenge. It would mean entering into a high-risk situation with an unclear future, no sense of permanence, no pensionable income and a lot of travel away from home. Annette was pregnant with our first child, Claire, at this time. There are some people who are driven by nothing but their career ambition. I am not one of those – my family has huge priority, and whatever I might undertake is a team effort with Annette. Everything is talked through together, and each of us has always acted as a buffer for the other in tough times. The sense of teamwork that we share means you never face a crisis alone and you know you have the unquestioning loyalty of the other throughout. It balances the boat in a storm.

Annette: My attitude from the outset was, 'Just do it.' It was a huge risk, but I had such confidence in Pat that I supported him no matter what uncertainty we faced. I remember going for a meal together one night and talking through all the plans. At the end of that meal, we decided that we were going to go for it. We felt we had nothing to lose and in the worst case could always start again with something else. I considered the possibility that we could face very difficult times, but I never countenanced the thought that Pat would not succeed.

I was excited because I saw it as a major opportunity. I even felt a childlike patriotism. I had been raised by Irish emigrants abroad and wanted to be part of an opportunity to reinvest in Ireland in a true spirit of progressiveness now that I was home. This was going to be the first ever Irish telecommunications buy-out. I believe we were at the forefront of a new Irish confidence. This buy-out was a clear example of Irish people's willingness to take over the management of a foreign company in the confidence that they could run it more successfully. This new confidence was also strongly apparent in my gender. For the first time, women did not automatically anticipate giving up work when they got married and had a family. Empowerment through education offered more choices. From Pat's perspective, there was a feeling that we could do this as well as anyone else, and I felt that he could do it better than anyone else. There are no obstacles when you are young and in love.

Pat did travel a lot, but when he was home, we knew he was home, and we did an awful lot together. In one sense, the departures and homecomings strengthened the relationship. There was little chance for us to grow tired of 'living in each other's ears'. The tearful airport goodbyes and the ecstatic 'welcome homes' with the children strengthened the bond. The sacrifices made then are reflected in and now justified by the results.

Pat: I approached venture capitalists in Dublin with little success. They wanted to deal with grey-haired managing directors, not a thirty-year-old. There was little appetite among the investment community in Ireland at that time for a technology company whose major asset was the intelligence of its workforce. We had little difficulty in raising the funds through a private placing with an investment bank in London. We managed to raise about $2 million from this source and agreed a buy-out with Mitel. We changed the company's name to Delta Communications, and we started doing some serious research and development in telephony systems and signal converters. One of our early products enabled conversion of rotary-dial telephone exchanges to push-button systems.

Turning the company around was a hard graft. We had early cash-flow problems, and our creditors put us under pressure. Part of the negotiated buy-out deal included a guarantee of $3 million worth of annual business from Mitel for five years. Eighteen months later, they scaled back their commitment and eventually cancelled it altogether, so we had to find revenue elsewhere to keep to our business plan. This was a particular blow to our confidence, and I recall spending nights on the phone to colleagues, trying to convince them that we could survive and that we had the ability and the guts to make it through the tough times. Many of them are still part of Tellabs and, I think, are the better for the experience. Their individual contributions made our subsequent success possible.

Succeeding together

We started with minimal revenues from our own products of $2 million per year and grew steadily to a stable, profitable $7 million in revenues two years later. After five years, the venture capitalists wanted to sell their stake of equity, so we went in search of a US partner that needed a strong presence in the European market. I whittled an initial list of potential partners down to two. Of these, Tellabs, based in Chicago, shared with us a strong belief in the importance of research and development. More importantly, they were genuine, good people. The Tellabs executives were approachable straight talkers with a high level of integrity. This was typified by Michael Birck, founder and CEO of Tellabs, who has remained a strong supporter and friend of our Irish operations. I could see that our management teams would get on well, identify good product opportunities and enable the business to grow in the right direction.

Tellabs purchased Delta Communications, and that relationship went superbly well. I remained head of Tellabs Ireland and became vice-president of Tellabs worldwide. The company has gone from strength to strength. Throughout the 1990s, we grew at a rate of more than 30% on average per year – a phenomenal rate. In 1999, Tellabs was the fastest-growing stock in the United States over the previous five years. Tellabs Ireland is one of the largest research and development centres in the country. In 1999, it won the overall National Innovation Award, sponsored by the government in association with PricewaterhouseCoopers and the *Irish Times*, for a telecommunications switching technology we created through our research and development facilities. The technology also resulted in the signing of a deal worth $100 million with Sprint International to integrate voice applications into its broadband platform. We employ 660 people in Shannon, 330 in Drogheda and plan a further expansion of the facility in Shannon in the near future. Tellabs Ireland had revenues of some $300 million in 2000. It has been an incredible journey. That is part of the reason I am still here today. There is no time to get restless with so much rapid change and growth happening.

Annette: As well as managing the growing business in Limerick, I launched a new centre for occupational health, called Abbey Physio, in the International Financial Services Centre (IFSC) in Dublin. Abbey Physio provides consultation services to companies on occupational health and injury issues. We have built an extensive company client list steadily over several years. We advise on the validity of personal injury cases and also advise companies on improving their office ergonomics, work systems and environment – everything from the optimal light and colour environment and desk layout to the best office dynamic for promoting employee health and productivity. Our greatest source of clients by far is North American multinational companies. Through Abbey Physio, I have researched international best practices in occupational health and, as a result, introduced to Ireland new technology for the testing of injuries. The software-driven technology is well received by individuals, companies and insurers alike and accepted in the courts. Returning people to work after injury is very satisfying, and challenging discrimination based on disability is something I feel strongly about. Fortunately, employers are well disposed towards adaptation of work practices for existing employees. Much work still needs to be done to educate employers on the issue of disability. Disability does not necessarily mean inability to work – it means rather that different skills should be recognized and appreciated.

Of all these activities – managing the clinics, research projects, lecturing, working with the multinationals – I cannot say which is my favourite. I love the variation that ensures I never get bored. I feel a bit stretched at times, but that is good for me. It makes me delegate and prioritize, and I retreat to the family to restore my energy when I need to. The flexibility I have through my ability to do certain work from home, such as writing reports or making calls, helps me to reduce the time I spend away from the youngest, who still needs encouragement to do his homework! To unwind, we travel together as a family. Family has always been most important, so we often make a holiday out of a business trip in order to be together. I think that we are successful in feeling contented and happy. Real success for me is in spiritual contentment, human relationships and family time. Our interests are not just in expanding careers or the acquisition of capital. We are both more interested in the type of community we want to live in and what we will pass on when we leave it behind. The best times we have are when we open the house to family and friends, take a picnic up to the lake at Killaloe or go to sports matches. For us, that is real time, real life, and we are fortunate that our work is fulfilling and provides us with the means to do these things.

Family and friends

Pat: Weekends have always been sacred family time. We spend time together, whether we are relaxing at home, outdoors at the lake or attending the kids' sports activities. We have a good work–life balance. That is probably the reason why we are not great at golf! If the priorities are family and work, then we have to forget about number three – golf. Playing sports is very rare indeed now, confined to holidays when we can carve out enough time. Someday we will have time enough to practise and get competitive.

I played a lot of rugby and still have my rugby friends and really enjoy going to matches. Sports, in particular team sports, are a great education for the workplace. I experienced being captain of one team or another and found the leadership I learnt on the field to be a great help in my career. The good captains I have known are rarely glory-seekers, but instead transform a group of individuals into a team, channelling the energy into winning. It is creating a shared sense of passion, working for each other and standing by each other that creates a winning team. Learning how to accept defeat with grace is also a skill for life. Our young son has learnt to fight back the tears in recent years and accept loss as a learning experience. He can take the knock of losing and resolve to win the next time. He recalls scores of matches played year after year, delighted to win, but not to win at all costs so much as to 'play fair to win'.

Annette: When Pat returned from England after four years, he togged out with his old Limerick rugby club for the first time since his absence. There were many new faces on the team, but within five minutes of meeting them in the dressing room, Pat was changing their positions and dictating the game plan. A lot of the new players wondered who this 'newcomer' was at all. Even still, they recall with humour their first meeting with Pat and are quick to put him in his place, reminding him of early memories of less than glorious games. He does not forget who he is or where he comes from, and as a testament to that, we have the same close friends now as then. Pat has always shown good leadership because he is inclusive and keeps everybody onside. He is a good listener, negotiates well and manages to orchestrate an outcome that works for everyone involved. He is generous in giving credit and is not politically motivated. He has negotiated very effectively on behalf of Tellabs Ireland, always seeking to strengthen the position of Shannon in the corporation. International colleagues always have a positive experience when they visit the Tellabs plant in Ireland to learn from the successful operations in Ireland, and we have made a lot of friends of many nationalities.

Leadership, enterprise and innovation

Pat: I have a strong commitment to Tellabs, but I am involved in a number of other companies as a director. I like getting involved in the early stages of new enterprises to provide experience and guidance. If I decide on equity participation, there is a heightened sense of excitement. Still in my mid-forties, I think there is plenty of time for many more enterprise opportunities. Sometimes I feel enterprise is in my blood. Some aspects of leadership can be learnt, but a deep gut instinct is needed to really exploit an enterprise opportunity. There has to be a feeling inside that you are right, when all around tell you otherwise. In my own case, naivety and bullishness co-existed in equal measure at times. I think that I have since matured and hope that my approach is more considered, less impatient and a little wiser than in energy-packed former times. I now derive tremendous pleasure from taking time to mentor and develop others. Many people with good enterprise ideas expect instant success, but it takes an awful lot of hard work, drive and personality traits such as passion and commitment to make it work.

Annette: I think a successful enterprise attitude is certainly personality-driven, but I also believe that it may be inculcated in children. They can be encouraged to believe in themselves and imbued with a greater self-confidence to be creative and enterprising. I love to see these attributes fostered. I love to see people with a purpose and a belief that they can make a difference. There are many people who want to improve their community through their enterprise, not for self-glorification but simply to feel a sense of contribution and achievement. I am privileged to have met many such people through my expanding occupational health practice and as patients in the clinic. They provide inspiration to my own work.

Pat: There is no shortage of leadership and innovation in the community around us. I was honoured to be invited to become chairman of the Regional Innovation Committee for the Mid-West. This initiative is funded by the European Union and has the objective of raising the level of innovation in the region. Innovation has always been a core value of mine. I have always tried to seek new ways to do things, whether it be developing a new product or service or addressing organizational issues. I have always believed that innovation is the root of economic development and growth. Innovation is much more than an enterprising idea – it is bringing that enterprise to fruition by generating revenue from a product or service in the marketplace.

The Regional Innovation Committee has made good progress in bringing the national agencies for industrial and enterprise development into a closer relationship with the education sector and regional enterprises. For a long time, the agencies have been occupied with distributing and administering grants to enterprises. This is going to change as the availability of grants is reduced. The relationship of the agencies with regional enterprise must therefore evolve naturally from that of being a 'banker' to one of being a 'broker'. Enterprises can benefit from the agencies' expertise and guidance in research and development, growth strategies and technology innovation.

A dramatic increase in the levels of innovation and enterprise in the region has taken place over the last fifteen years. There are enough case studies demonstrating real enterprise success to inspire a new confidence in the people of this region and indeed throughout Ireland. Venture capital institutions and banks understand that the environment is conducive to enterprise and that a supportive infrastructure for enterprise is in place – it is a time of great opportunity in Ireland.

Responsibility

Annette: And yet we need to maintain a sense of responsibility. Accumulation of wealth is not the be-all and end-all. Those who achieve the lucky breaks – receive a good education and enjoy a comfortable environment – need to look beyond their personal circumstances and commit themselves to improving the broader environment to which they belong. Two hundred thousand people in a poverty trap is a reality, and no amount of complacency can erase that. We need to empower more people by bringing them into the fold of the community and facilitating their contribution, each according to his or her own ability, whatever that may be. My work brings me into contact with many who have fallen through the cracks of the overstretched health services or suffered through a lack of rehabilitation services for the short-term disabled, many of whom have unfortunately become more disabled through lack of appropriate intervention.

Pat: Irish companies can help to fulfil this responsibility. Furthermore, Irish companies have an opportunity to promote an enterprise culture of openness, honesty and integrity. I have a feeling that Claire, Fiona and Rory will all work in an enterprise environment, and I would like to see them in the embrace of that culture. I hope they never know the fear of failure, which so often holds us back. So much can be learnt by mistakes. Our society needs to adapt to the prospect of enterprises failing without recrimination. There is a cultural shame attached to failure that must be shed if further enterprise is to yield deserved successes. Those who have succeeded in this new Irish economy and who can give their most precious commodity – time – can impart tremendous knowledge to the next generation. In this way, succeeding generations can build on what has been achieved and create a better environment to live in.

Annette: The extra effort to create a healthy environment is paid back tenfold. Life is so short – one gains so much enrichment from doing things well and so much pleasure from seeing people achieve their potential. We will make mistakes, but we can learn from them. We have a tremendous opportunity to realize an Ireland that will be the best possible place to live in.

BRODY SWEENEY

Founder and managing director,
O'Brien's Irish Sandwich Bars

*T*he homely welcome at the Dublin headquarters of O'Brien's
Irish Sandwich Bars is a reflection of the care for people that
Brody Sweeney has instilled and shares with his colleagues. His
unassuming openness and down-to-earth style allow him to relate
easily to people of all kinds. Brody Sweeney is perhaps the
quintessential people's man. He believes that people are good and
puts his faith in simplicity.

Yet success did not come easily to Brody Sweeney. Indeed, for
a decade and a half he struggled merely to survive in business. One
enterprise initiative after another failed, leaving him heavily in
debt. Through these years, his passion to succeed drove him to
overcome the financial pressures and disappointment of business
failure. This passion was fuelled in part by fear and in part by a
belief in his ability to achieve his greatest ambitions. That self-
belief has prevailed, and in making a success of his enterprise, he
has gained a better understanding of himself, people and life.

His franchise business, O'Brien's Irish Sandwich Bars, is
flourishing. It has doubled in growth every year since 1996. More
than 120 outlets span Europe, the United States, Asia and
Australia, and there are firm plans to continue the current rate of
growth and expand the product range under a highly visible brand
name. That name conveys an image of young, healthy and
contemporary Irishness to its domestic and international

customers. Internationally, according to Brody Sweeney, that image is the coolest thing around.

Passion

There is a great passion in the team of people who work with me. There are twenty-five people in our central office looking after the worldwide franchises, and every one of them is fired up about making a difference and achieving the best they are capable of. The passion swells by its own momentum – it is contagious in O'Brien's. I never have to let anyone go for not making his or her best effort. If someone is not pulling their weight, the others in the team will not put up with them – a slacker will be ousted and dispatched. The passion grows from a shared vision at O'Brien's of being youthful, energetic and, at the same time, entrepreneurial. The passion would be compromised if our central office grew too big and bureaucratic. A large office environment can engender conservatism, incompetence and lifelessness. We have several hundred people working with O'Brien's around the world, but you will find no superfluous layers of middle management here.

People

In the heart of Dublin, the buzz of the city centre fuels enthusiasm. It is far more adrenaline-inducing than being enclosed in an office park in the suburbs. On the practical side, there are a lot of O'Brien's outlets in the vicinity, and the owners can come in and see us easily. But more importantly, I love the city because I am closer to people. People walk in to this office from the street to chat about the possibilities of starting an O'Brien's sandwich bar. Most of my time these days is consumed with meeting people and interviewing them as potential franchise owners. Most people are good people. However, a lot of people are simply not suited to running a sandwich bar. For instance, many retired couples come to me with the thought that it would be lovely to spend their free time running an O'Brien's, and I have to break it to them that it is not a good idea.

Sometimes I meet people who want to bite off my arm. They expect to be told that they are the right people, that they cannot go wrong, that they will make a million quid and never look back. They expect to be signed up and protected. I do not find it hard to respond. I tell them the truth – that it is a major life investment and a lot of terribly hard work. I tell them that they cannot have the franchise and that we will not sell it to them, chase them or ever ring them. Those who say 'I still want to do it' are the people we want. One of my team will bring a candidate for a casual lunch and a walk and gauge the candidate's interest and personal attitude. If candidates have a healthy outlook on life and a sense of humour, as most people do, I like them. If they indulge in any racial prejudice or misogyny, I have little time for them.

There are two sides to running my business. The first is the technical side – the way a store is designed in terms of fittings, lighting and décor; the advertising and marketing that promotes our business; and the financial accounting that monitors the health of the business. The other side is the people side – the motivation of people through a shared vision that makes them get out of bed in the morning; the expression of a bright outlook for the future; and the support and positive interaction between people who work together. We can create a technically brilliant and beautifully designed product, but ultimately, we are in the hospitality industry, and if the people side is not healthy, the business will not work.

I believe that people tend to attract other like-minded people. People who share the same values and behaviours feel comfortable working together. That is why it is important to me that we foster a company culture in which people are treated with respect and dignity. Everybody is placed on an equal footing. There is little room for politics or hierarchy at O'Brien's. I want to see this culture shared with new staff and with suppliers and franchisees so that it permeates the organization.

When people join us, they share the common vision at O'Brien's, they buy into the honesty of hard work, and they buy into me. The people we enlist are the most important part of the formula that makes O'Brien's a success. Indeed, on a national level, I believe that people are our greatest asset. Our ability to communicate with an inherent warmth and intimacy is a gift. Irish people are sincere, trustworthy, hard-working and can talk through any difficult situation. At O'Brien's, the understanding relationship that we maintain with our franchise-holders is the bedrock of our business.

Simplicity

Simplicity is at the very heart of our operations. There is no need for complicated management systems. We generate a strong team spirit by ensuring that people have a sense of involvement. The franchise concept is extremely simple and can be easily replicated. We produce top-quality food and beverages and consistently give the customers what they want. The vast majority of customers are in the 18–34 age group. We want to offer them an ambience to which they can relate while maintaining a unique identity. We try to use Irish food suppliers where possible and carry high-quality Irish products such as Darina Allen's Ballymaloe Relish, Lily O'Brien's hand-made chocolates, and Irish Whiskey Salami in all of our stores. Our outlets have a contemporary, clean design with modern Irish art and music. We have a youthful, in-house designer team managed by Stephen Knight. Orla Kaminska produces the finest hand-painted tiles for our stores, and Nigel Swan displays atmospheric photographs that highlight the contemporary feel. In fact, I have a great interest in the ability of photography to create an atmosphere, and O'Brien's sponsors an annual Photographer of the Year competition in association with Fujifilm.

The franchise mechanism is also simple. Holders need to produce £30,000 to £60,000 in personal investment capital and arrange an equivalent amount in financial support. We arrange site selection as well as architectural design and fitting of the shop on their behalf, and we offer back-up management and competitive analysis. We provide advance training and continual support and guidance once the franchise is established. We earn our money from licence fees and royalty on sales but have no up-front capital exposure.

We have now opened over 120 outlets around the world and have just signed deals to open 30 more in Asia and 30 more in Australia, while a further 60 are planned for Britain. The busiest outlet in the world is in Dublin Airport, and the second busiest is in Blanchardstown. My favourite locations are the five outlets in Singapore. The Singaporeans cannot get enough chicken and bacon triple-decker sandwiches. I invented that sandwich myself and tested it so much in early trials that I have not been able to eat another one since. When the *Riverdance* cast played in Singapore, they had lunch at an O'Brien's Irish Sandwich Bar before every show.

The Irish brand travels very well and conveys an image of health and good living. We love promoting our Irish image abroad, but the image alone will not sustain business. Repeat custom accounts for 90% of business. People return to buy our sandwiches because of the quality, service and value for money they enjoy. I am under no illusion that 40 million Irish-Americans will call into our stores because we are Irish. As we expand into new countries, the mix of our own business ethics with those prevalent in some countries can pose new dilemmas. It is important to us to adapt our outlook to match different cultures, but certain countries present grey areas in relation to what we ourselves perceive as important ethical issues, such as child labour. I hope we can be a force for change for the better in the countries in which we operate.

Hard times

Most of our outlets are working swimmingly, and we are looking forward to strong growth in the years ahead. Life was not always so. The first fifteen years of my working life were overshadowed by recession. I never knew anything but hard times, never knew anything but surviving. Forget profit – that concept never came into it.

I started my business career working with my father. He secured the Irish franchise for the Prontaprint business services and reproduction shops. I was in college at the National Institute of Higher Education taking business studies at the time, but I simply did not enjoy the academic life and was glad of the opportunity to abscond. Soon after its introduction in Ireland, Prontaprint was perceived to be successful. We increased the number of outlets throughout the country, and the trademark bright shopfronts portrayed a sanguine existence. In truth, we never, ever made any money.

My Dad and I struggled for eight years to make the business profitable, but we were never able to achieve the margins or scale that were needed to make it viable. After eight long and difficult years, my father died. I felt that I had had enough of it, so I sold the franchise and left Ireland for the United States. I went in search of new business opportunities and spent time with different food chain outlets, such as Popeyes and Little Caesar's. I studied how the Americans were applying the franchise concept and effectively learnt the trade a little better from the inside. It was an invaluable education.

I came home to Ireland with a hunger to apply what I had learnt. I met up with a friend who was thinking of opening a sandwich bar on Merrion Row in Dublin. I had a clear idea in my mind that we could take an existing product that everybody buys – the sandwich – improve it, use the best-quality ingredients available and design a clean, attractive and modern environment in which to sell it. The prospects for business looked slow, but my appetite was whetted and I devised the O'Brien's Sandwich Bar concept – 'Healthy, contemporary, top-quality Irish sandwiches'. I opened the first outlet in the city centre on George's Street. I was fired up to overcome the failures of the past. I could see the O'Brien's brand growing to emulate the fame of Guinness. I was consumed almost by a blind arrogance. It was a disaster! It was 1988, the back end of the recession, and we were too early for the market of high spenders that exists today.

At that time, corner shops sold the traditional, drooping ham-and-cheese sandwiches for 50p, with ham you could see the light through. We started selling generously overflowing sandwiches for £1.50, and people could not fathom paying that much for a sandwich. Now, of course, people part with £3 for a sandwich without a flicker of thought, and we have forty city-centre shops in Dublin to facilitate them, but in 1988 the population was not ready for us. Every year, for six years, we lost money, and every year we lost more than the previous year. It was a frightening time, but I could not get off the track I was on. You can lose an awful lot of money before you realize how deeply in crisis you are. I was in terrible trouble with everybody. I should have stopped with the banks but kept sinking deeper into debt. I retained a belief that I was 'alright', that it would all work out in the end but would just 'take a little longer' than I had originally thought.

I married my wife, Louise, during this time. Financially, it was a bad time to get married. There was no honeymoon, and the present we had received of a microwave went straight into the business. We could manage to put bread on the table, but there were no perks such as holidays. We had a strong relationship, and Louise was a tremendous support to me. I felt bad that we could not go out on a Friday or Saturday night with friends – we were either working or exhausted. In any case, we started a family and had young children that needed to be looked after at home. Children have a great levelling effect because you start to think about them more than yourself and your difficulties.

I felt that if I stopped working in the business, I was dead. As long as I continued to trade, there was always hope that I would turn the corner. I felt that there would be an end to the problems if I worked hard enough and kept ploughing forward. That is what I did – just kept going. There was nothing brave about it. It was simply that the alternative was too hard to contemplate. The alternative was to go bankrupt, have my loans called in and be put out of my house and home. Throughout 1991, 1992 and 1993, I was under terrible pressure. There were many sleepless nights and tears. It was horrible, but the only other course was to admit defeat and walk from the table – how do you tell that to your family?

After six years, I had three shops in business, each in trouble. I had learnt from Prontaprint to stay comfortable with a small number of outlets and not to expand beyond my capability, so I decided to work hard on improving the business of these shops. I always believed that I could make a success of them and imagined that they were part of a pilot series of outlets. I looked on my task as one of ironing out the bugs and experimenting with different marketing strategies and products so that when the chain became successful, I would have a process that would work every time I pushed the buttons. I prepared everything I needed to have in place for a successful future franchise. I drafted the franchise agreements and legal documents. I wrote the operating manuals. I drew up architectural designs for new shops. I even outlined food specifications as detailed as estimating the water, salt and fat content of the ham we would serve. Perhaps I devoted all this energy to avoid acknowledging a fundamental flaw – all this time, the money was flowing in the wrong direction. Another person might have given up. I never allowed myself to believe that the losses the shops made were funds flowing in one direction only. I invested all the time and energy and passion I had to turn the business around. Slowly, painstakingly, we turned that corner and started making a profit. It had been a long fifteen years of losses, failure and learning. I set out with a youthful arrogance that I could achieve greatness and got dragged through the reality that life is not as easy as I imagined. It was a long time to live on fear, hunger and passion to overcome the problems, but in the end, I made it. I would not wish it on another soul in a million years.

Conquering Britain

These days, I have a new energy and a desire to travel and open O'Brien's outlets in more countries and meet new people. With over 120 outlets worldwide and an annual growth rate of 100%, I will have plenty of opportunities for fulfilment. I want to make the O'Brien's brand as strong as Starbucks in the United States or as Prêt à Manger in London. I do not see why O'Brien's cannot become as big a brand as McDonald's. Interestingly, we operate under the name of Brody's in the United States. When we set up our first O'Brien's franchise in Chicago, where there are tens of pages of O'Briens in the phonebook, another O'Brien's restaurant threatened to sue us. Brody's is a little more unique and still has an Irish ring.

Our strategy for brand expansion is simple. When an outlet starts up, 85% of business comes from people who work or live in the 500 square yards that surround it. We start by conquering the market in that 500-square-yard area. Then we reach out to the wider district through advertising. We target new locations and stretch our brand to cover a whole city. Then we begin to spread to other cities. In Britain, for instance, O'Brien's is now the most successful sandwich chain in Glasgow, Edinburgh, Manchester, Cambridge and Plymouth. Liverpool and Birmingham are our next city targets, and eventually we will conquer the market throughout Britain.

The disadvantage of dealing with Britain is the absence of the euro currency. The euro is a great benefit to our business in mainland Europe. We buy a lot of our refrigeration equipment in Italy and our lighting equipment in France. The elimination of transaction costs for currency exchange at banks amounts to significant savings for us. We have paid a lot of attention to ensuring a smooth transition from old to new currencies and have a well-made plan for overseeing the dual-currency period. The reduction of individual currency volatility that the euro brings means that we have one less risk to take account of in our business planning.

Opportunities and expectations

The advantage of the current strength of the O'Brien's brand is that my young team could now survive without me. They have an ingrained self-sufficiency that is found in most young Irish people today. There is a huge optimism and pride in Irish people. There is also a great confidence and security in terms of finding work that makes the attitude of joining a company for life redundant. Many people are using their newfound wealth in good and charitable ways. They have not forgotten that despite Ireland's status as a very wealthy country, there are many social shortcomings that need to be addressed. I believe there is still a distinct difference between 'haves' and 'have nots' with regard to the opportunities they have to raise their living standards in this booming economy. Less privileged people can more often be caught in the constraints of their environment. At the same time, what they see and hear of this boom through the media raises their expectations of what life can deliver.

Many social evils have stayed with us through the boom. There are a shameful number of people struggling with poverty throughout the country. Young kids addicted to heroin sleep on the city streets at night. Young families struggle on small farms scattered throughout the countryside, trying to maintain a subsistence living and investing in farm products that cannot enable them to compete with the farming economies of scale in Eastern European countries on the threshold of joining the EU. Despite the recent wealth creation, these problems remain with us, and they are hard to resolve. The government has a great responsibility to address social problems. However, it is also in the hands of Irish citizens, communities and companies to make a difference. Why should we always look to an arms-length administration to solve the problems that we share as a nation? I believe companies have a tremendous opportunity to make a difference as employers. They can offer work to people from less privileged districts and create a bubble of opportunity to raise living standards in that district. A therapy for poverty is hope. Hope is in a job and a wage.

Hope and positive encouragement

Hope feeds on a positive attitude to people. People from less privileged districts are fed a constant barrage of negative sentiment: 'Get a job; you are in trouble with the police; you have no future.' If every Irish company took a person from such a district, they would be offering the positive encouragement that would make a real difference. The young people would see the bright possibilities of the future, feel a sense of integration and contribution and break out of the negative conditioning that locks them into the trap of poverty.

I believe that Irish people who have been successful are starting to adopt this approach and are reaching out. A minority of people who benefitted from the newly wealthy environment have raised their own living standards without giving back to their community. They are indulging in a pace of life that is so much faster than in the time of my parents. I am starting to sound like my father . . . I got on great with him.

As a parent myself, I know how powerful positive encouragement can be. I am reading a book on parenthood that illustrates how easy it is to resort to negative language:

'You're late'; 'You can't go out in that'; 'You haven't done your homework'; 'I don't like that fella you're hanging around with'; 'Get up to your room and tidy it, it's a disgrace'; 'You've shown no respect to your grandmother, you haven't rung her in ages.' How many households have resounded with this talk? Positive encouragement makes for a far better atmosphere.

I am glad to have received a lot of positive encouragement from my own parents when I was young. I was never very strong at my academic studies when I was at school at Blackrock College, and I was encouraged to try other, more enterprising initiatives. I started my first business of cutting down trees when I was fifteen. I gathered six people to work together during our summer holidays, and we won a contract to cut trees in Killiney in south Co. Dublin. We were making very good money until, one day, we cut a tree that fell into a road and on top of a car. The fire brigade was called, there was a war of trouble, and eventually we were thrown off the job. A year later, I started a company called Southern House Minders. I gathered some more friends who wanted to become plumbers or painters or carpenters, and I advertised their services door to door. When I secured a job, I would send the team in to do the work and take 10% commission from their pay. Conceptually, it was a great idea, but the guys did not do the jobs properly, we had no insurance, and there was a rake of phone calls upsetting the household. My mother eventually got irate at the size of the phone bill at home, so we folded the business. As a kid, I was always looking for the next idea to make a buck rather than keeping my head in the study books.

I have two godchildren with mental disabilities. They are no different to me than any of my other godchildren. Some time ago, I saw a documentary on television about the Special Olympics and Ireland's successful bid to host the

Games in 2003. The Games are the flagship of the Special Olympics – an international, year-round programme of sports training and competition for people with learning disabilities. The documentary highlighted that Denis O'Brien would chair the Irish Special Olympics Committee. I wrote to him the next day and asked if O'Brien's could get involved in sponsorship. We were invited to join the corporate sponsorship team as one of five main commercial sponsors and have committed to raising £1 million. This is the most enjoyable and satisfying project I have been involved in to date with this company. Through our O'Brien's outlets, we have prime access to customers to get them involved in fund-raising. I am happy to part with our marketing budget to raise awareness of the Special Olympics. Our staff love the idea. Fund-raising has become a shared goal of franchise owners around the world. This is strengthening relationships within the company and creating goodwill with our customers that translates into commercial benefit. The Special Olympics of 2003 will be the biggest sporting event that year. The international focus will be huge. O'Brien's international franchises are being encouraged to support their respective national Special Olympics teams. At home, we will encourage our Irish franchise staff to participate as some of the 30,000 volunteers needed to run the Games' day-to-day operations and also provide the catering. More than 7,000 competitors from over 160 countries are expected to take part. This will be the first time that the Special Olympics Summer Games will be held outside the United States, so there will be a lot of international focus and interest. I have no doubt that the 2003 Special Olympics in Ireland will be an event to be remembered.

Life

I love my life now. I know myself better. I am good at what I do and will carry on for years, because I love it. I continue to be a positive thinker and rarely let things get me down. My positive outlook is what allowed me to continue through the hard times, but I am the first to acknowledge that I am incredibly lucky. I also know what my weaknesses are. For instance, I am not good at multi-tasking, so in terms of my business interests, I stay focussed only on O'Brien's. That does not mean that we cannot be creative with the O'Brien's concept. O'Brien's outlets are located on the busiest high streets, resulting in a highly visible brand. We can exploit the strength of that brand in many ways, from selling a current range of O'Brien's consumables that includes not only sandwiches but also bottled water, chocolates and cookies to selling future products as diverse as holidays, perhaps. If I did not earn a wage, I would still come to work every day. My natural curiosity would drive me to find out the latest news. I am a bit of a gossip. When I have been away for three days, I get excited to see which friends have e-mailed me in my absence.

I live life at my own pace, and I enjoy it that way. I am not a workaholic at all these days. I take lots of time off and head to the west of Ireland with my wife, Louise, and our four children. We have a cottage and a little boat in Sligo, and I am happy there. I am passionate about boating and fishing – they give me a great sense of contentment. However, I still get my greatest fulfilment from the people in O'Brien's. I love most meeting someone who wants to open a franchise and is terribly daunted. They realize they are making a major change in life and are afraid of the risk. I say to them, 'Trust me, it will work out.' Then, together, we invest our time and our efforts and our hopes and our fears, and together we make it work out.

LOUIS WALSH

Band manager and pop music promoter

*L*ouis Walsh spurns the self-important image that one might expect to find in a band manager who has achieved such phenomenal worldwide success as he has in the last seven years. In its place is a comfortable and laid-back attitude that is rooted in his small-town childhood. He fosters the same down-to-earth attitude in the pop acts he manages, and it is undoubtedly this lack of pretension that ensures the stunning and continued success of acts such as Boyzone, Westlife and Samantha Mumba.

Louis Walsh learnt the trade of his chosen enterprise the hard way. On leaving school, he did his apprenticeship in the Irish showband scene, running errands while learning the intricate workings of the music business. He made a scarce living for many years, promoting Irish bands that hoped in vain to emulate the success of a few Irish rock legends. To change his luck, he decided to rely on his own enterprise and rebuilt Irish pop music in a matter of years. He created Irish pop bands that fulfilled their primary objective – to entertain. Despite criticism of the credibility of his acts, Louis Walsh fashioned and marketed bands that took Europe, Asia and the United States by storm, broke music industry records and placed Ireland on the world map of pop music.

An ordinary life

I am from Kiltimagh in Co. Mayo. The world in Kiltimagh was small and parochial. The town had a church, a supermarket and countless bars. We lived on Chapel Street, and there was little money at home so that life growing up was very ordinary. I am the second oldest of a family of nine – a family of good, ordinary people. Most of my family left home for Dublin or America. All but one, my brother Joseph, have returned to Ireland to settle down. I have two brothers that keep me company in Dublin – Frankie is my accountant, Éamon is a policeman – and the rest of my siblings have returned to Mayo. I could never settle in Mayo. I love the west of Ireland on a good day, but on a bad day when the skies are dark and the weather is bad, I could not live there. I have left life in the West behind. The culture there revolves around the pub, football and politics, and I have no interest in any of these things.

I had a great time growing up because of my love of music. It was my escape from ordinary life. I loved everything to do with music and spent my days dreaming of escaping Mayo to work in the business. I bought every music magazine in the town shops and read every related article I could lay my hands on. I spent countless hours in record shops listening to my favourite songs. I listened to everything but loved the music of soul artists such as Marvin Gaye and Al Green the best. Ella Fitzgerald, Frank Sinatra, Dusty Springfield and Patsy Cline were great favourites of mine as well.

I was absolutely useless in school. I was not an academic person at all. My mother thought I might become a priest because I was the eldest boy, so she sent me to boarding school at St Nathy's College in Ballaghaderreen, Co. Roscommon. I lasted all of three years there and was far from a model student. I was bored, did not like the strict regime, was not interested in sports like most students, performed poorly in exams and hated the food.

In many ways, it was a good experience for me, because I decided with a passion that I had to make something more of my life, and I gained a strong sense of independence. When I failed my Intermediate Certificate, the school principal advised my mother not to waste her money by sending me back. So I left and went instead to day school at St Patrick's College in Swinford. I took the bus for the few miles from Kiltimagh every day and had a great time there. I just scraped by academically and was lucky to pass my Leaving Certificate.

My first job after school was working in a bar in Claremorris, Co. Mayo. With a population of 2,500, Claremorris was three times larger than Kiltimagh but still a far cry from the bustling cities I was dreaming of. There was an easy-going pace of life in the town, which nestled into lovely countryside of rolling drumlins, eskers, woods and lakes. The bar was owned by two brothers, Frank and Vincent Gill, who also happened to be members of local showband The Royal Blues. The brothers introduced me to their manager, a Dublin man called Tommy Hayden, and he must have sensed my eagerness for the business and thirst to go to Dublin, because he offered me a job. I was delighted at the opportunity and moved to the city.

Tough game

I worked as a gofer in Tommy Hayden's showband office. I made tea, answered the phones, ironed shirts for the band members and cleaned the office. I knew all the great showbands and handled the fan mail for Red Hurley, the Royal Showband and the Nevada Showband. I stayed with a sister and slept on the floor of her apartment. I did not care that I was earning hardly any money, because I knew I was learning the business from the bottom up. I learnt all about the Irish music business – how to book bands, promote them, get their records played on the radio and get good reviews published in the newspapers. Tommy involved me in the booking of bands, and it was great training, because I made some terrible deals and had some bad years but learnt from every mistake.

When the disco scene came, it killed the cover showbands. I started to make my own deals in the music business with rock bands. I worked with some great artists like Rob Strong and Brush Shiels and bands like In Tua Nua, The Power of Dreams and Cry Before Dawn, promoting their music and booking live gigs. None became very successful. Several very nearly hit the big time but could not make the leap when stardom beckoned. Many good bands handled the pressure of expectations and their own aspirations badly when they got a record deal. No Sweat thought they were overnight rock stars from LA, but they were really from Galway. Aslan had a few good early songs but believed they were Spinal Tap.

I started to get involved with Irish *Eurovision* contestants such as Johnny Logan and Linda Martin. I booked some fantastic venues with them, but the money was always tight. In truth, I was a struggling agent and was just about paying the bills. It was such a hard time that I find it difficult to think about and harder still to express. The promoters I dealt with were terrible people. Contracts meant nothing to them. I might book a band for a gig in Donegal for £1000, and if a poor crowd showed, we would not get paid. We would have hired all the sound gear, dragged ourselves across the country to a dark hall with damp walls, a tin roof and no dressing rooms for changing and returned home late the same night, weary, disgusted and empty-handed. I was making 10% commission on gig fees, which was often 10% of nothing. That was the nature of the business. It was a tough game.

I was at the bottom of the barrel in the music business. I had tried everything I knew, and, to be honest, I had nothing left. For a while, being in business for myself seemed like a bad choice. Entertainment was my chosen enterprise, and I found it hard to make enough money to get by. However, I had always dreamt of being in this business and I was not going to give up for lack of determination and hard work. I kept searching for that one band or that one great idea that would give me the break I wanted. If it were not for Boyzone, I would never have survived.

Boyzone

The story of Boyzone will make a great movie some day. I was managing plenty of rock bands that were all trying desperately to be like U2, but one in a million was getting through. I decided it was time to create a band myself. I watched the progress of British boy bands like Take That and East17. These bands had stormed the charts and whipped up teenage hysteria at concerts as a result of brilliant marketing. I thought they were entertaining, but I thought that a young Irish band could do as well, if not better. For some time, I did not have the nerve to try the concept, but the more I thought about the idea of creating our own Irish boy band, the more I believed I could make a success of it. I had very little help and few resources at the outset, and nobody seemed to believe in the idea. I knew I would have to build the idea and the band myself, and with no money, I knew it would have to be on a shoestring. Looking back, I am glad I did it myself. If things had been handed to me on a plate, I might not have achieved as much as I have.

At the end of 1993 I arranged to hold a grand audition in Digges Lane in Dublin and started advertising the fact that I was looking for the best Irish talent for a new boy band. On the day of the audition, 150 people turned up, and 90% of them were really terrible. I chose some good singers from the rest and decided to work with these to create the band. The boys I chose were great characters. Shane Lynch had been trying out his singing voice while working as an apprentice mechanic in his dad's garage. He had always wanted to be a pop star, and as soon as I saw him, I knew he had the potential. Everyone else did three auditions, but I signed him up after just one. Stephen Gately was used to a little limelight, as he had been acting and modelling from the age of sixteen. He had made a small appearance at the beginning of the film *The Commitments* and was ready to give up his job as a sales assistant in Makulla's clothes store and go for a full-time career in entertainment. When I heard Ronan Keating sing, I fell off my seat. He was confident, looked good and had an excellent voice. At sixteen, Ronan was still in school, although he worked part-time in a shoe store called Korky's and helped out in his mum's hairdressers. I wanted to put him on a different career path, and he was more than happy to take the chance. Mikey Graham was working as a mechanic when he tried out at the auditions. I turned him down initially, but because he was so determined to make it in the music business and had good experience singing with cover bands in Dublin, I decided to give him a second chance, and he has worked out really well. I first saw Keith Duffy dancing on the stage at the POD nightclub in Dublin, and I asked him to come to a second round of auditions for the band. He had strong presence and had worked as a doorman at several Dublin nightclubs. He decided to put his architecture studies on hold to take a shot at show business. The most important thing that they all had in common was that they really wanted to make it. They were ready to put in very hard work for no reward in the beginning. They had that burning will to stretch for greatness and the positive attitude to make it happen. As a manager, the right attitude is worth more to me than fantastic talent. These boys had the looks, the personality and the talent, and they wanted to work like hell. They had star quality.

As the auditions took place, the media took a subtle interest, and the *Late Late Show* gave us the opportunity to perform live for the first time. It was a fantastic chance to be on the biggest national show in Ireland, and the early exposure was a great coup. The only trouble was that the band had never performed together. I had picked the boys on a Thursday night, and they were on the *Late Late Show* on the Friday night. They dressed up in boiler suits and did a live number they had rehearsed only hours earlier. A lot of people derided their attempt, and the critics gave them no hope, but, in retrospect, they showed great courage and belief in themselves and had launched their music careers in front of hundreds of thousands of people.

I started to generate support from people who could help me. John Reynolds, manager of the POD, gave me £10,000 to make a first single in Britain, and I secured a local deal with Paul Keogh of Polydor records. For months, we worked extremely hard. The boys trained their voices and learnt how to dance. Longs hours in small studios built chemistry and a sense of fun that would help them survive for so long. We released the first single, 'Working My Way Back to You', in May 1994, and it reached number 3 in the Irish charts. Boyzone took to the road, crammed into a little white van, travelling the length and breadth of Ireland to drum up a groundswell of support. They played small, backwater gigs week after week and slowly built up local credibility and professionalism. By the end of the year, they were ready for their first major concert in the enormous Point Theatre in Dublin. Thousands of kids came to the concert screaming and went home screaming. I never thought they would be big outside Ireland. At the start, I had hoped that perhaps we would achieve a top thirty hit in the Irish charts, but when their second single went to number 2 in the UK pop charts and they won the *Smash Hits* award for Best New Act shortly afterwards, I believed we were onto something big.

We worked extremely hard marketing the band and touring to build a big fan base across Ireland and the United Kingdom, and the band finally achieved their first number 1 in December 1996 with 'Words'. Boyzone have gone on to have six number 1 hit singles and three number 1 albums in total, and they became the first pop act in history to make the top three with their first fourteen singles. They achieved a solid level of credibility when they won the prestigious Ivor Novello award for the song 'Picture of You', and the Record of the Year award in 1998 for 'No Matter What'. In 1999 Boyzone won the Best Album award and the Best UK and Ireland Act award at the MTV Europe awards. That is hard work paying off. That is success.

The Boys have done great things in their careers. They have travelled across the world and performed throughout Europe and Asia to huge audiences. They have been ambassadors for Ireland and the Irish music industry. Through all this, they have remained down-to-earth boys from Dublin city. They have always been streetwise and aware of the business around them. If I had the chance to start over, I would pick the same five guys because the fun side of their personalities has always shone through and we have had a great time together. If you were to meet them and knew nothing of their singing career, you would say they were really nice guys – that is their secret. They tell me their most special moments have been at small concerts, such as when they played two shows for the Omagh Fund for victims of the bomb and their families. They met 150 young people injured by the bomb and donated the platinum disc they received for sales of 'No Matter What'. After five years at the top of the charts, the boys are starting to look in different directions and pursue individual projects. Each is trying solo music releases. Mikey has tried his hand at small acting parts,

Shane races rally cars for Ford, Keith has a host of modelling offers, and Stephen has presented the *Smash Hits* Poll Winners' party.

Of all the band members, Ronan has emerged as the most successful solo artist. He always displayed a natural leadership in the band from the early days and often acted as spokesman for the others. He has a natural charm that fans and media love, and he has that X-factor of appeal that is so hard to describe in words but easy to see in action. When Ronan walks into a room, he creates a special impact – everybody turns their heads. In 1997 he co-hosted the *Eurovision Song Contest* in Dublin with Carrie Crowley, and later that year MTV asked him to present the MTV Europe awards. Ronan presented the Miss World competition in 1998, and in 1999 he again hosted the MTV Europe awards from Dublin. He has also presented a talent search show on the BBC called *Get Your Act Together*. Ronan has been successful at everything he has put his hand to. These events placed him in front of hundreds of millions of viewers and were a tremendous platform to launch a solo music career that I now manage. More important than this exposure, however, was Ronan's commitment to hard work. He is a driven young man.

Commitment and business

I can only manage people who can show me the commitment to achieve greatness. I open the doors for a music act, get as much TV and radio coverage as possible, market a good image and work with the media to generate support, but after that, it is up to the act to make it happen. If the band or the individual has less than 100% commitment and does not have the work ethic and attitude that I need, I would prefer to work with the next band that does. The Carter Twins are a case in point. They were great singers and nice people, and I felt sure we could create a success with them. They were similar to a British duo, Robson and Jerome, that had made it big in America. I worked hard for them and won them a record deal, but they did not have the spark or the commitment to make it work out. They left me and have not been heard of since. If I work with an act that is totally dedicated, I will do everything possible to promote them. We may have disagreements, but if the fundamental commitment is there, we will always get along.

I do not see myself as a particularly talented businessman in the conventional sense. I am no good with figures or finances. That is not what gets me out of bed in the morning. I am driven because I enjoy what I am doing. I did not make a lot of money in the early days, but I continued because this business is my life. I like it in the same way that a CEO of a technology company likes his business or a bank manager of a bank likes his. I love the fact that I can put a band together, make a hit record and make them famous. In some ways, my business is about turning groups off a conveyor belt. Manufacturing the whole package is what I am good at.

Westlife

What Boyzone achieved in five years, Westlife has done in less than two. As in any business, I have learnt with experience, and I do not repeat the same mistakes. Once I knew how to manage one boy band, I could manage another successfully. Westlife was originally a group of six lads from Sligo. I came across them first in 1998 and immediately liked what I saw. I decided to co-manage the boys with Ronan Keating. The first action I took was to cut three of the group out and add two new members from Dublin. It was hard to cut out three from the original group, but I think it was the right decision. An analogy I often think of when selecting the right members for a new group is that I am like a football manager who tries to field only the best possible team.

There can be no passengers. The three Sligo boys are Mark Feehily, Kian Egan and Shane Filan, and the Dublin lads are Nicky Byrne and Bryan McFaddan. Shane and Mark have the best voices I have ever heard in the music industry. No one in the world comes close to the quality they have. The others also have great voices, and the combined talent is fantastic. They work harder than any other pop or rock band in the world, promoting themselves 24/7, and they deserve the success they have enjoyed. That success has been phenomenal. The group's first single, 'Flying Without Wings', entered the UK charts at number 1. They have gone on to score a massive seven consecutive number 1 hits, equalling the industry record set by the Beatles. Their first album, Westlife, went gold and platinum, selling more than a million copies worldwide. At the MTV Europe music awards in 1999, *Westlife* swept the board, winning six awards, including Best Album and Best UK and Ireland Act. Westlife was the first of my acts to make an impact in the United States. The record companies never pushed the buttons for Boyzone, but they are behind Westlife and want them to reach the top of the cross-Atlantic charts. Cracking the US market is a personal challenge of mine. With a population of 250 million, the rewards can be huge, but it requires a big investment of time and energy.

Samantha Mumba

After Westlife, I decided to try managing a big individual act. I met a stunning girl one night in the VIP room of Lillie's Bordello nightclub in Dublin. Accompanied by her mum, she had sweet-talked her way into the VIP room, pretending to the bouncers that she was a New York R & B singer. Apparently, she knew I was there and wanted an introduction. When I met her, I knew she had the quality of a star. At the age of only fifteen, she already had a super confidence, charm and natural beauty and seemed to me like a young Janet Jackson. I told her there and then that I wanted to manage her. We swapped phone numbers, and I called her mother the next day. When I heard her sing, I was convinced that she had a great future in the business. She had already proven her determination, and her training between the ages of three and fifteen with the Billy Barry Kids stage company gave her an edge of professionalism. I contacted my associate in Polydor records, Colin Barlow, and he agreed to see her without even previewing a demo tape, something unheard of in the music industry. When he saw Samantha, Barlow was convinced we had a superstar on our hands, and we sent her to Sweden for coaching with top producer Anders Bagge, who could create the right sound and image for her. We started working on a first album before Polydor had even finalized a contract, so that we could launch Samantha's career as soon as possible. In June 2000 we released the first single, 'Gotta Tell You', which went to number 1 in Ireland and entered the top ten in the United Kingdom and the United States. She sold a million copies worldwide and created a feverish reaction in the United States, where record companies fell over each other in a race to sign her. Samantha was invited onto every major US chat show coast to coast. She has such a down-to-earth style in her interviews and is so full of life. Her second single, 'Body II Body', a great pop song with an R & B flavour, also went to number 1 in Ireland and the top ten in the United Kingdom and fuelled interest in her rising stardom. She was signed by L'Oréal for the New Face of L'Oréal campaign and was offered several acting opportunities in major films. She turned down a role with Will Smith in a film about Muhammad Ali but took the offer of a role in a film with Jeremy Irons and Guy Pierce that will be released in 2002. It is early days for Samantha – she has a huge future. I am just glad and lucky to be managing her.

Pop music

Each of these great artists is diverse in their own special way, but ultimately, pop music is a business. I am in the business of selling. It is no different from selling a product like tea or coffee, except that I believe in what I sell. I believe in the kids as if they were part of my family. I invest so much in my acts and work harder than people could imagine. I get very nervous when a new act makes a debut. All the months of dedication, hard work and endless communication with the record companies come to a head. I knew without a doubt that Westlife were going to be great, but I was still restless and nervous on the eve of their first ever gig. It is extremely hard to become successful, but it is even harder to stay successful. Once they have made it to the top of the charts in the music business, they are up against the best in the world. They are competing for that top spot all the time, and only one song or one album can be there. Despite the pressure at the top, I believe there is always room for an inflow of new and fresh talent. There is an endless market demand for good pop bands. People try to dissect and understand the nature of pop success too much. The argument of whether my pop music is credible is often raised in the media. There is no need to analyze it. Good pop music is entertainment for kids, and they buy the records if they like them. My bands have taken on the world and earned results commensurate with the enormous effort they have invested.

The market for different sounds is very wide, and I hope to exploit the full spectrum by covering everything. I am starting a new rock band that will be similar to the 1980s group Duran Duran but will not compete with Westlife. I will soon go on a countrywide tour of Ireland to spot new potential pop music acts. There is a wealth of talent in Ireland that is just waiting to be given the chance to conquer the world, and I hope to find some of it before the big record companies that have flocked to Ireland in recent times swallow it all up. Young Irish people have a great work ethic that makes them wonderful to work with. I love the attitude in Ireland – people are prepared to give anything a go and work hard enough to make a success of it. It is a characteristic that stands out in the world. I would not live anywhere else. When I am in London for a week, I cannot wait to come home. I like Los Angeles and could live there for a few months of the year, but I would miss home and the Irish attitude.

I get thousands of tapes to review from hopeful young people. I have had some great successes, but for each of these, there have been countless shattered dreams. The music business is one in which the record companies take control of artists, so I would advise any aspiring musician to get a good manager and a good lawyer and read as much as possible about the nature of the music business before launching headlong into it. A pop career is a short career. If they make a little money, they should realize that it will not last forever. The greatest Irish musicians have withstood the pressures and retained their freedom. Among these, I admire Dolores Keane, Enya, Sinéad O'Connor, Brian Kennedy and my very favourite and one of the most influential in the world – Van Morrison.

The greatest kick I get is seeing a band I manage go to number 1 in the charts. I want to achieve more number 1 hits than any manager ever has. So far I have nineteen – one with Johnny Logan, six with Boyzone, eight with Westlife, two with Ronan Keating and two with Samantha Mumba. I am not in the business for the money. I am here because I love what I do. I love the music in my life, I love living in Dublin, and I can pay the bills. I always believed that I could make something of my life and be at least moderately successful. I never wanted to be a big fish in a small pond. If there is one lesson, it is that if it has worked for me in Ireland, it can work for anyone.

CAROLE WARD

Body artist; Founder and manager,

the Bodyartist Company

Carole Ward's studio, in the heart of Dublin city, is split through the middle. A curtain runs diagonally from one vertex to its opposite. One side has the charming chaos of an overflowing, theatrical prop room, with feathers, masks, hats and sequins strewn about. The other is completely bare except for a warm blue carpet on which Carole's live models will undergo a creative metamorphosis.

Carole Ward is an artist and a businesswoman. She expresses her artistic creativity by way of the Bodyartist Company, which she established from a personal nadir of unemployment. She decided that she had endured enough stagnation from a cycle of dependence on social employment schemes and chose to take control of her life and her future.

That Carole Ward has established herself as one of the world's most popular body artists and made a success of her business is a credit to her talent and her enterprise. That her art is in such great demand in Ireland today is a reflection of the changing tastes and growing sophistication that accompany a new national prosperity and confidence. There is a new inclusiveness in attitudes to art: patrons are increasingly open to novel art forms, and they now have the wealth to indulge their artistic interests. The majority of Carole's customers are large Irish and international companies – companies that are contributing not only to a new national *economic prosperity but also, in this case, to the promotion of one particularly captivating art form.*

Natural artist

I always wanted to be an artist. From the age of two, I found myself indulging in creative and artistic activities. I found myself surrounded by creativity at home. My dad had a wonderful manual dexterity. He was always building things for our house and home. He used to make these beautiful, measured hand-sketched drawings – they were very simple and very precise. There was creative talent everywhere. My mother constantly made clothes for her children, my aunt was a tailoress, and my grandmother owned a clothes stall in the old Liberties market, so between them my two brothers, two sisters and I enjoyed the height of homemade fashion. I do not think they particularly enjoyed making clothes, but shop-bought articles were so very expensive, and they turned out marvellous matching sets for us all, including my brother!

By the time of my Intermediate Certificate, I felt sure that I wanted to go to art college once I had finished school. In anticipation of getting the right school results that would allow me to pursue third level education, I should have been concentrating on my academic studies for exams, but found relief and diversion in art. I took art classes three nights a week through my school years. When I eventually finished secondary school, I managed to secure a place at the National College of Art and Design (NCAD) in Dublin to study fashion.

NCAD has a tremendous history. For 250 years, the college has seen the growth of, and the changes in, the visual consciousness of Irish culture. In the late eighteenth century and into the nineteenth century, the college trained many of the artists, apprentices, designers, painters and sculptors whose talents helped to shape Georgian Dublin. In the late nineteenth century, the college was a centre for a crafts revival, attracting as students W. B. Yeats and A. E. Russell, among others. NCAD fosters the traditional artistic skills, while remaining open to new developments in art and design. For instance, the Faculty of Fine Arts provides courses in painting, printing and sculpture that help students to develop an individual way of seeing and interpreting, and of expressing themselves visually, while the Faculty of Visual Communications provides courses that develop skills in film, photography and multimedia that can be applied in the advertising, fashion and information technology industries.

My first year at NCAD was superb. The intensity of being surrounded by so many like-minded people was great, and the college looked after us very well. We had the opportunity to embrace and experiment with many different and novel art forms. Then suddenly, I became quite lost in the subsequent three years of my course. The college moved premises to an interim building, before finally settling at a new campus location in Thomas Street, and there was a sense of upheaval. I am a person who likes things to be well organized. I like structure and regularly draw up lists of 'things to do' in order to organize my time efficiently. I find it difficult to focus in a disorganized environment, and as a result, I did not specialize in a particular field in my art studies. Whereas I aimed at first to concentrate on fashion design, I lost my appetite for simple pattern-making. I was frustrated with the open-ended atmosphere, and, in fact, I found it hard to recall my sense of focus even when I graduated in the early 1980s.

Drifting

Eighty students graduated from my class in 1981, and good work was scarce to find. Finding work as a delivery person in a graphic design studio was considered to be a lucky break at that time. I found myself drifting from one community arts group to another working as an arts administrator. I worked in the administration of women's, film and theatre events in the Grapevine Arts Centre, the Project Arts Centre, the Quay Co-op and the Centre for the Performing Arts, where I was also the information officer. I was involved in the production of the *Irish Women's Diary and Guidebook* and produced the Women As Advertised touring exhibit. Lastly, I also administered, publicized and toured with three theatre shows with three different casts and travelled to twenty-four first-time venues. I enjoyed working for these groups, but I felt I was not developing artistically during that period. However, I did learn how to manage administrative records and organize artistic events, and I also learnt useful customer-oriented skills such as making presentations and establishing networks.

My final arts administration job was with the Project Arts Centre. I was let go by the Project Arts Centre in 1991 to make way for social employment workers. Unemployment was something of a shock to me. I signed up for several different social employment schemes. I tried various state-sponsored schemes whereby I would undertake community-based art activities. I gave workshops to adults and children on theatre make-up, commercial art, mural- and face-painting. I produced murals in two northside schools and one in James Connolly Memorial Hospital in Blanchardstown. The matron at the hospital, Rose Coyle, was an endearing woman who organized for the mural to be painted and gave me all the support I needed. The mural was located in a section of the hospital devoted to elderly patients, and I painted a lush rose garden with climbing wallflowers against which people could sit. Soon after, there was a rumour that the hospital would be demolished and relocated from its prime property spot. Rose Coyle liked the mural so much that she promised to save the wall and take it to the new premises. Between these schemes, I signed on and off the social welfare payment system, the dole. By participating in the schemes, I was not an official unemployment statistic, but in reality, I did not have a job.

Creative enterprise

I decided that the next project I undertook would be one into which I would throw my full energy and imagination. I would single-mindedly apply myself to a new project and pull myself out of a cycle of schemes that may not have led to any worthwhile personal or artistic development. Most of all, I wanted to use my talents constructively to take control of my future.

A friend asked me if I would do some children's face painting in the Ilac Shopping Centre in Dublin. I agreed to try it and was determined to overcome my natural shyness of standing in the middle of a busy shopping centre with a handful of paints and brushes. On the day I started, I became totally engrossed in the face-painting from the very first minute. Three hours after beginning, I stood up straight for the first time. It was so busy. I loved the painting and relating to the children, and I loved being able to control my day. To my surprise, I found that I made more than three times as much money in a day of face-painting as I had earned in my arts administration job.

Suddenly, the idea that face-painting could be a source of business took on a whole new momentum that dragged me willingly along. I appeared on an RTE television programme called *How Do You Do?* I also tried face-painting on Dublin's busy Grafton Street, charging £1 per child. One day, out of the blue, a party organizer came up to me on Grafton Street and asked me if I would attend a children's party to paint faces. The party was for the daughter of the U2 guitarist, The Edge. It was a lot of fun. I started to create a portfolio of photographs of my work and showed it to *In Dublin* magazine. The editors assumed that I did full-body painting when they saw the portfolio. I certainly had the idea for full-body painting but had never tried it. The *In Dublin* editors asked me to paint a model's body for a front cover. I was delighted. I had the freedom to use my imagination on something very different that the magazine was prepared to gamble on. The work was a three-quarter-body painting on the theme of the Statue of Liberty. *In Dublin* magazine then commissioned me to paint another front cover during the soccer World Cup. I painted Sylvia Myers, one of Ireland's top models, with the impression of a football on her chest and a billowing Irish flag around her body. When people saw the cover photograph, they could not believe that it was just a painting, because it looked so real. My confidence really grew when I won a body-painting competition at the RDS in Dublin, sponsored by Annie Cribben of Make-Up Forever. That was the first time I had ever painted a full body. These successes made me realize that I could create a whole new source of business from body-painting.

I was excited about the prospect of starting a body-painting business and determined to make a success of it. I wanted to turn my life around from being sporadically unemployed to being successfully and more contentedly self-employed. However, I first decided to take a step back and prepare for a business launch in a level-headed, organized way. I decided to follow a FÁS business scheme that lasted two months. At the end of this scheme, I knew how to register my business and set up a business account. I was quite computer-literate, which was helpful in organizing my administrative activities. I even made my own business cards. After the FÁS course, I went on an allowance scheme that provided ever-decreasing payments that helped with my initial start-up and advertising costs, which might otherwise have been prohibitive. I began by working from my own home. As demand for my work increased, I realized that I needed more space, and I soon moved into a studio in the heart of Dublin, on Wicklow Street. This was an important move for a couple of reasons. Firstly, it brought me closer to the centre of commerce and business in Dublin, so I was more accessible to customers. Secondly, I had a base and a professional studio that gave me the credibility that I needed to convey. The Inner City Enterprise Group, which assists unemployed people to initiate new enterprise activities in Dublin city, helped me with an early rent subsidy.

Being self-employed

The support from these different sources has been tremendous because it has allowed me to become self-sufficient. I had the financial support to overcome early costs and the psychological support of knowing that I had encouragement and backing. I am very happy to be self-employed. I have control and can be creative. My direction and speed of development are in my own hands. I have a strong sense of self-motivation and energy from running my own business. I am doing the thing in life that is most important to me.

Being able to run my own enterprise is life-sustaining. There is a feeling of stability in my life and a feeling that at last I fit.

I have found a positive sense of identity instead of being at the mercy of forces beyond my control. I have progressed from feeling disoriented and fragmented to feeling motivated and in command of my abilities and talents. Now I have a basis for self-expression, not only in my art but also at a simple social level. People's attitudes are far more attentive and appreciative when I tell them about my work. At parties, I can say, 'This is what I do, this is what my life is about.'

At the outset, the challenge of running my own business was a little scary. There were particularly quiet times when my work was in short demand or an expected opportunity did not come to fruition. For instance, an intended television documentary on my work fell through. These things can be frightening in small ways. Sometimes it is easy to forget all that I have invested in my enterprise, so that each day is like starting afresh. My portfolio looks like a seamless continuum of work, but, of course, it does not show where the gaps of activity have occurred. Throughout the quiet times, I tried to keep busy and maintain an enthusiasm in my heart. I developed my ideas and prepared and planned for the future. Eventually, the phone would always ring, several jobs would roll in together, and I would be buoyant with work.

I have achieved very positive recognition as Ireland's first full-time body artist. In the last few years, I have established a list of more than 100 clients. Besides magazine covers, film and television work and fashion shoots, my work is very popular at major corporate events, such as the launch and marketing of a new product or company. I create a great diversity of characters. As well as that for *In Dublin* magazine, I have created a Statue of Liberty for Waterford Crystal, a snake for An Post and a water sprite for Marathon Sports. A human statue I created for Ulster Bank's millennium party gave many guests a real fright when it moved. I love to see people's reactions to my body art. That is the culmination of my work. Most people have not seen anything of its kind before. They look quietly from a distance, sometimes with an elusive smile.

Many Irish computer software and information technology companies, such as Indigo and Eircell, and several international computer firms, such as Gateway and American Power Conversion (APC), have used my body art to promote products that tend to be hard to present visually. For instance, software that is embedded in a disk or a microchip and hardware that is fashioned into an obscure piece of mechanical equipment is difficult to promote in an eye-catching way. I can help to advertise a futuristic information technology message, for example, by painting a model or group of models in an imaginative way.

The cost to me of creating a full-body painting work starts at £300, and materials or any props are an additional cost. When I embark on a project with a company, I put great effort into agreeing a design that the client is perfectly happy with. I make several designs that we discuss together and tailor to the exact need of the client before deciding on the final product. Then I make templates out of acetate, paper or card and make hats and body garments so that everything is ready for the painting event itself. More than two-thirds of a project takes place before the model sets foot in the studio. A full body takes some five hours to paint on my own, and I keep a very strict time schedule, painting different parts of the body as I countdown to the actual photocall. The model has to be extremely patient. In fact, my friends and family get the top award for patience, as I use them for practice runs. I now have a family album with a difference. I have a photo of my brother-in-law with a painting of the Mona Lisa on the back of his head.

While the work is painstaking, it is never, ever boring. After all, I am working with a beautiful canvas – the 2 square metres of the human body. I choose paints from an array of water-based body paints in forty different colours, and I use some forty different glitters sourced from every corner of the world. I like to emphasize the line of the natural body shape by using hats and other accessories for dramatic effect. When I have finished the painting, I simply enjoy standing back and watching the photographers capture the result. Meeting people is another enjoyable part of my work. I like to relate to other professional creative artists, such as photographers, creative designers and choreographers. Some of the models that I work with are brimming with personality and are a lot of fun. I enjoy meeting the managing directors of companies at a promotion event and young entrepreneurs at start-up events. Often I meet well-known celebrities at events to which they have been invited for publicity. I encounter the most inspiring people through my work. These are the people who have a kind word of encouragement about my work, and that is uplifting. People who understand me and treat me well leave the greatest impression.

World recognition

My work has taken me around the country, and recently I worked with world-renowned milliner Philip Treacy in London. As the film and music-video industry grows in Ireland, I would like to get involved in creating stunning new characters for the big screen. I also have ambitions to expand the business internationally and take advantage of the international standing that I have earned. According to the world Internet ring for body artists, bodypainters.com, I am the fourth most popular body artist in the world this year. My website records over 11,000 hits each month. Potential clients visit to view my portfolio of work, and many people log on just out of interest and to explore the many colourful photos of past work. There is an intrigue about the idea of painting a body that captivates many people. Body-painting underwent a rebirth in modern times in the decade of the 1960s. It became very popular on the French Riviera. While lounging on the beach, rich residents would indulge in the novel pastime of painting and being painted. Body-painting also found its way onto the cinema screen in the 1960s with such dramatic images as the Bond girl in *Goldfinger*.

As I have built up the business, I have extended my work into a huge diversity of areas. Along with the countless corporate events that I have covered, my body-painting has appeared in forty-three newspapers, three magazine front covers and several television commercials and programmes, including RTÉ's *Glenroe* and its Olympic coverage in 2000. I divide my body-painting into four sections: Fantasy and faces; Half-body painting; Full-body painting; and Hats. I have an extensive list of models that includes dancers, fire-eaters, professional models and mime artists who hail from Sudan, Nigeria, Morocco, the Philippines, France, the USA, Wales, England and Ireland.

I spend about one-third of my time taking care of administrative aspects of my business – banking, raising funding and developing my online business. Another third of my time is spent creating – designing and painting. The remaining third is spent in outreach – visiting potential customers and promoting my work. I trawl through my networks to uncover possible new clients. I read the newspapers to see what events are taking place in the near future and approach the sponsors to whet their appetite for my work. I try not to miss an opportunity. Recently, as I walked through St Stephen's Green, I came across the music group Westlife while they were undertaking a promotional shoot. I walked up and asked for their PR manager, to whom I gave my card, and I suggested that they might use my work sometime. There is nothing to lose and everything to gain, especially if I make it easy for people to get in touch with me. Being responsible for my own enterprise and livelihood makes me bold enough to seize every chance to develop that enterprise.

Living art and enterprise

Body art is a living art in a very real way, but sometimes I think the art has a life of its own. The increase in demand for body-painting has been such that at times I am forced to turn work away. Now I pass much additional work to assistants on a job-to-job basis. As a result of the surge in the economy, the demand and turnover of business has soared. The boundaries of image-making are being stretched also. The images are becoming more avant-garde – what might have been eye-catching several years ago is easily overshadowed by even more powerful images today.

To me, there is no paradox in being both artistic and involved in enterprise. There are imaginative and creative aspects to both. Since I live in both spheres, I am certainly sensitive to peer artists being exploited in a business world. As a sole trader in my discipline, I decide on both the art and the price. Artists who live only for the art in their minds often find themselves exploited when they make the transition to the world of fixing a price for their art – a great dilemma. It is a shame that people who are born with a special artistic talent must struggle with a general undervaluation of that talent and the poor wages they are likely to receive in a commercial environment. I would be miserable if I myself were a cut-throat and demanding businesswoman. I want to achieve balance and harmony between the artistic and business aspects of my life. I live in a harmonious environment in the Guinness Ivy Trust apartments for artists. It is a beautiful red-brick building curving away from Bride Street in the Liberties towards Christchurch. I am surrounded by other artists, writers and actors. It is like a microcommunity in which we quickly dispense with the superfluous 'weather talk' and discuss each other's art and techniques. We share what is new in the art world and which Irish art events are coming up. It is a perfect environment that allows us to learn from each other.

Irish creativity and diversity

Irish people certainly have creative flair. However, I do not think it is right to see Irish people as being any better or worse than any other race. Extreme self-appreciation is too close to a narrow-minded nationalism to which I do not subscribe.

If Irish creativity has produced storytelling and literature that the world admires, that does not make us superior to another race. It simply reflects a difference in the environment in which the creativity has been shaped. For instance, there is an argument which states that the reason we have a tradition of great Irish writing is because we had neither the money nor resources to be theatrical. In the same way, our climate has held us back from creating parades as spectacular as those the Brazilians have. In Ireland, as in every country, we are shaped by our environment and limitations. This nature of being limited by our environment is a bond between nations that is in fact stronger than the differences we more often celebrate.

Ireland needs to grow in tolerance and appreciation of cultural diversity. I am often embarrassed by the way in which many people treat immigrants. Instead of being curious and open enough to embrace a new culture, many indigenous people are afraid of the unknown and shun diversity. I ask myself what indeed 'indigenous Irish' actually means after so many waves of cultural invasion and assimilation in this country. As a body artist, I love working with different races and skin colours. I appreciate the beautiful, consistent tone of dark skin.

Creativity can certainly be fostered in Ireland through active encouragement. I find encouragement works best with young people. When children show creative talents, they should be supported in a way that allows their creativity to blossom. A simple 'Well done' lightens the heart and generates a positive energy that helps to develop a talent. I recall from my school days that I was talented at art but terrible at the Irish language. I remember feeling very guilty about my lack of proficiency in Irish and failing to realize that my natural ability lay elsewhere. Encouragement of natural talent rather than being forced to conform to a required academic curriculum would lead to a healthy lessening of pressure. Today, schools do in fact promote a greater number of non-traditional academic activities such as transition-year community projects, which are very worthwhile as preparation for the real world beyond the safe confines of the school gates. I think encouragement of creativity needs to be sensitive to different gender requirements. Boys and girls simply think differently and relate to the world differently. No matter what part of Ireland I happen to be in, when I ask a child what he or she wants to be, the answer is the same. A girl wants to be a princess, and a boy wants to be a monster.

In the 1980s, when feminism gathered momentum through the start-up of many new women's groups, I had a great deal of exposure to gender-specific thinking. I find that Irish men and women react differently to my body art. I find that women are open to and at ease with a fresh approach that exposes the form of the human body in a way that is interesting in itself. Men tend to be more interested in who the model is.

One episode at a corporate marketing event was quite funny. To mark the launch of a DVD product, I painted a model with silver metallic panels, exposing openings of sinew. Dressed in silver hot pants that were a little outrageous, she stood with great beauty and elegance in a business reception area. She was captivatingly stunning, and her painted skin simply radiated. When several businessmen in dark suits crossed the reception area, they shuffled to a halt in silent amazement. Their only comment was a tentative, 'Did you see her shoes?'

Whether men and women react differently to fine art or not, as opposed to decorative art such as body painting, is more difficult to say. I can only speak personally. I am not a fine artist but a decorative artist who paints graphics on the human body. I once had to decide whether to pursue fine art through my life drawings or not, but I decided it was not the right area for me. I prefer the decorative art of making attractive things look more attractive. I love the fine art galleries because they are quiet spaces. I do not seek great depth in a work of art. I like to see how it has been made. I am simply interested in how materials have been arranged to improve their original state.

In a way, that is the best description of my own body art. My body art is also a momentary work. I will spend hours creating an effect, only for it to be washed away later. A photograph of the work will consign it to permanent record. There is also permanence in the way that I will always feel lifted by the recognition I have achieved, by the fact that I am making the best use of my talent and by the knowledge that I overcame the daunting challenge of starting my own enterprise and succeeding with it.